The Art of Achievement

Neil McLennan & Kevin Murphy

The Art of Achievement

Mastering Skills for Success in the Modern Marketplace

First published in 2014 by lulu.com

First published 2014
By lulu.com

All rights reserved

Copyright © Neil McLennan & Kevin Murphy 2014-The right of Neil McLennan & Kevin Murphy to be identified as the authors has been asserted by them.

All rights reserved. No part of this publication may be reproduced, stored or introduced into a retrieval system without the prior written permission of the authors.

ISBN 978-1-291-86742-8

To Daniel, who had friends in books.

'Employ your time in improving yourself by other men's writings, so that you shall gain easily what others have labored hard for.' **(Socrates)**

Contents

	Foreword	Colin Dalrymple	xi
	Making your life a masterpiece	Neil McLennan & Kevin Murphy	xiii
1.	The 'Big Four' Partner	Blair Nimmo	1
2.	The Commonwealth Games Athlete	Jayne Nisbet	10
3.	The Chef and Restaurant Owner	Craig Wilson	20
4.	The Life Scientist	Nicola Stanley-Wall	31
5.	The Tourism Director	Leslie Vella	42
6.	The Doctor	Angela Davidson	53
7.	The Media Producer and Director	Keith Girdwood	63
8.	The Care Sector Executive	Ruth Smyth	73
9.	The Third Sector Recruitment Executive	Alan Surgeon	85
10.	The Military Officer	Paul Wilson	97
11.	The Painter and Decorator	Barbara Hastie	106
	The End of the Beginning	Kevin Murphy & Neil McLennan	115
	Further Reading		117

Foreword

So much emphasis today is placed on the importance of skills. It is very appropriate following the success of 'Determined to Succeed' that Neil and Kevin should wish to continue to highlight how successful individuals have used their skills to achieve distinction in their field. Once again these well-respected authors have resisted the temptation to produce a technical piece of work, preferring to re-employ their winning formula of allowing others to tell their own stories so we can learn directly from them. The result is a fascinating and enjoyable series of journeys, each demonstrating that the path to success and the *'Art' of Achievement* can have many different starting points.

Where 'Determined to Succeed' explored the skills required to succeed, this next 'chapter' (for there will surely be many more!) explains how a number of high achievers have succeeded in their chosen careers. What is more, each of the contributors has offered insights into what he or she believes will be critical for success in any future marketplace. These are not predictions, but observations based on their own experiences – many of their 'critical success factors' are remarkably similar to what we might expect in the current marketplace but with a few surprises along the way.

The structure of this book is as pleasing as it is simple. It reads like a series of personal stories and is accessible to any level of reader. Nor is there any pretentiousness to the book. It can be read for leisure on the morning commute or studied with greater scrutiny by those keen to delve deeper into the skills discussion. There are no 'one-stop shop' solutions or 'technical' advice on how to master skills – simply a brief résumé of contributors' experiences and what has worked for them.

What readers (be they students, educators, career changers or lay) will find, however, is commonality in the journey of each contributor. For even though these individuals come from a diverse range of backgrounds and have an equally diverse range of careers, there are a number of common themes running through their stories: hard work; interpersonal skills leading to reputation building; resilience; self-development; a recognition of the importance of teamwork; a willingness to continue to learn; and, flexibility.

It is also interesting – and heartening – to learn from the experiences of this group of high achievers that academic brilliance at an early age is not a prerequisite of later success. For, in the words of one, *'The concept of education only really begins for some once they leave school'*. Each of the interviews confirms that while all have strong self-belief and a determination to succeed, many also recognise the importance of maintaining a healthy work-life balance. Each appreciates that there is no need to be defined by the job(s) that he or she does, but rather they themselves are able to define their role by bringing their own individual skills to bear. What all our contributors also show very clearly is their passion for the work that they do, with most recognising the importance of giving something back in gratitude for the support they have received along the way.

This is a group of 'ordinary' people who have achieved, and continue to achieve, extraordinary success. Many have had to overcome obstacles on their journeys and have displayed remarkable resilience in their efforts to overcome difficulties in both their working and personal lives. Together, their stories demonstrate that there are many different approaches to mastering the skills required for success, both now and in the future.

This is a very easy read and will be welcomed as a natural follow-up to 'Determined to Succeed'.

Colin Dalrymple
Chief Executive, Scottish Training Federation

Making your life a Masterpiece

Neil McLennan & Kevin Murphy

'I have learned that success is to be measured not so much by the position that one has reached in life, but by the obstacles which he has had to overcome while trying to succeed.'

(Booker T. Washington)

The publication of our first book, 'Determined to Succeed' (2013), was largely motivated by our desire to stretch the 'skills debate' into the practical realities of the modern workplace and explore the core elements of what makes individuals succeed in their chosen careers. Having self-published the book, we had no real expectations regarding its sales or impact; we were simply interested in charting the career paths of successful people and believed that career starters/changers and educators might be interested too. A year on, we remain amazed by the response 'Determined to Succeed' has had.

In retrospect, perhaps we should not have been so surprised. The format of our book is unique. With no third party commentary or oblique references we simply asked successful people about the skills they use and how to acquire them. We used language that everyone could understand. Perhaps most importantly, we interviewed people who from inauspicious backgrounds have worked to distinguish themselves from the crowd.

'Determined to Succeed' was quickly adopted by educational institutions across the UK as a source of great insight into the modern marketplace. The skills it highlighted as being crucial were not those that could necessarily be learned in the classroom. Indeed, this extra-curricular focus appeared to be an area that many similar publications had failed to address. Neither a collection of autobiographies nor a self-help book, 'Determined to Succeed' was seen as an invaluable practical guide to mastering the human element of success. The emphasis the book placed on interpersonal skills - specifically, listening to and understanding others - is testament to this perspective. These were also the two main skills that we as authors employed to gain the information we needed to compile our book and draw out its key messages. To our knowledge, there are no educational institutions in the country offering classes or seminars in how to master these skills.

The success of 'Determined to Succeed' has also opened up debate on skill development *within* the marketplace. As authors we have both led seminars in the public sector on skill development and have been asked to contribute comment pieces to journals and newspapers. Excitingly, our learning has also led to huge demand on us to undertake speaking engagements. Most notably, we are repeatedly engaged in the private sector and specifically on many occasions by the world's largest professional services firm to speak to its executive and national recruitment team on how best to develop staff and highlight individual areas of excellence.

So, you may wonder, what led to the publication of our second book, 'The Art of Achievement'? Quite simply our readership demanded a sequel!

Although we are proud of 'Determined to Succeed', in some ways it felt incomplete. We had touched upon a broad range of careers but had not addressed many other core areas of employment such as food and drink, tourism, life sciences, the finance sector, care or creative industries to name but a few. We were also aware that events concerning the economy, questions on the role of the European Union, and the independence debate within the UK had raised fundamental uncertainties about the world in which we work. Our response was therefore two-fold: to interview more people from a core range of careers and to focus on what it will take to be a success in the *future marketplace*.

Following publication of our first book a number of organisations and individuals approached us, keen to offer case studies. Again we were careful in our selections, making sure that those who were *invited* to be part of the publication had recognised credentials and the ability to tell a story from which others could learn. As a result, we are delighted to say that the calibre of contributors to our second book is outstanding. In it we hear from, amongst others, Senior Partner of KPMG (Scotland), a former major in the British Army, an international athlete and a world champion tradesperson. Most importantly, they all have something unique to say.

As authors it is difficult to predict where this publication will take us. As a reader I would argue that it is entirely predictable: apply only a fraction of the learning expounded in this book and you will rapidly accelerate your career advancement, skill development and ultimately your ability to achieve!

Neil McLennan & Kevin Murphy

Chapter 1
The 'Big Four' Partner

Blair Nimmo is a senior partner with KPMG, one of the largest and most respected professional services firms in the world. KMPG are one of the 'Big Four' companies offering audit, assurance, tax, consultancy, actuarial, financial, legal and corporate services.

Specialising in corporate restructuring, Blair has over thirty years' experience advising businesses across a range of sectors including banking, oil and gas, and construction. He is a member of the Institute of Chartered Accountants of Scotland.

In addition to his client work, Blair also takes a keen interest in developing staff in KPMG. The restructuring practice that he leads has been the dominant market leader in Scotland for over twenty years, and is a reflection of the competitive drive and pursuit of excellence he instils in all his colleagues.

When I was asked to contribute to this book on skill development, I could not help but be drawn to an occasion a few years ago when I was invited back to my old school. The brief was simple: as a 'successful businessman' I was to give a presentation to pupils about my career and hopefully provide some inspiration for their own development. Returning to school after thirty years, my mind inevitably cast back to a younger version of myself and to my English teacher at that time who told my parents I would be 'lucky to achieve a 'C' grade in O-level English. His remark came to form the basis of my presentation. Whilst at the time I did not agree with him, he was certainly correct in stating that I showed no early signs of the success I would go on to achieve in business.

I did not come from a privileged background. I went to a state – not a private – school. I was not a prize winner in academics or sports. I was not the head boy or class representative. Instead, I was shy and self-conscious. Put simply, I was 'Joe Average'. Thus the very fact that achievements in life are not pre-determined but come about through hard work and seizing opportunities when they appear became the theme of my presentation. You can shape your own destiny once you commit everything you have to making your goals happen.

Incidentally, you may be wondering if I bumped into my old English teacher again? The answer is yes, he was sitting in the audience and I did take more than a little pleasure in proving his early assessment of me wrong!

Three skills for success

In a thirty-year career you may think it difficult to identify three skills that have been central to achieving my goals. In some ways this is true, but there are three that jump out more than any others: *initiative*, old-fashioned *hard work* and *interpersonal skills*. I shall discuss each of these skills in turn and demonstrate their effectiveness during key phases in my career. I will then discuss some of the themes that I believe will be crucial for success in the *future* marketplace.

Initiative
I never had a burning intention to be a chartered accountant or insolvency practitioner. Upon leaving school I could not even have described what these jobs involved. I was not sure what I wanted to do with my life. I chose business studies and accounting at Edinburgh University,

largely because my family advised me that this would be a good career move and lead to a well-paid job.

Truth be told, I found the academic side of university tedious. Not unlike many young men who leave home for the first time I was more interested in parties and girls! That is not to say that I neglected my studies, but again I certainly did not stand out when it came to academia. Nevertheless, representing my school and county at badminton I quickly developed confidence from the fact that I knew I could be good at *something*. The shy, self-conscious boy slowly changed into a more outgoing young man. With this change in personality I gradually pushed myself out there, started becoming involved in new activities and consequently got invited to parties where I met more people and made new friends. I was beginning to create momentum in my life in the direction I wanted to go; I was mastering the skill of taking the *initiative*.

For me, *initiative* is about proactively making things happen rather than being reactive and letting things happen to you. At the time I did not know it, but the skills I was learning at university through meeting and socialising with others would serve me well in my later career.

Leaving university with a fair but not outstanding degree you may be surprised to learn that I did not go straight into an accountancy firm. Instead, drawing on the interpersonal skills I now enjoyed using I worked as an area salesman for a local sports company in Edinburgh. It was a job I enjoyed because I was travelling throughout the country meeting new people and developing sales skills, which were essentially a mix of listening and being able to communicate with a wide array of new people, through my *initiative*. I also learned the important business skills of managing a diverse team of people, working hard and often how not to run a business.

Was this experience a waste of time? Whilst it may not have been the profession others would have chosen for me, especially after four years at university, I did value the important life skills I was acquiring - the *initiative* to go out and meet new people, and achieve sales targets. This ability to identify and seize opportunity worked well when the sports company I was working for suddenly went bust.

Faced with an uncertain future I decided to revert to what I knew and sought a position with a large international accountancy practice specialising in restructuring (or insolvency as it was called then). Interestingly, unlike my peers this was a position I would not have won had I applied straight from university: my academic grades were simply not good enough. In the years I spent working as a salesman, my friends from university had taken the formal route straight into 'safe' accountancy roles. My path was different. I had shown *initiative*, been exposed to a wide range of people and worked in an environment where I was responsible for driving and attaining competitive sales targets. These skills were valued by the practice, which would go on to give me the chance to study for a formal accountancy qualification. In terms of technical accountancy experience I was a few years behind those whom I had graduated with by the time I was offered a position, but the *initiative* I had shown in my time since university was soon to set me apart.

Hard work
Did I miss my sales job? The answer is yes, but I was smart enough to recognise the opportunity this new training contract presented. Coming from a family that was not well off and where my father had bounced around many jobs, I understood the value of job security and realised I had a lot of life ahead of me. I was also aware that I was now working alongside some seriously intelligent and driven people.

Perhaps because of the perception I developed of my academic ability at school, I did initially feel a little self-conscious about whether I had what it took to make it in my new environment. My response? I simply resolved to work harder than anyone else and refused to accept second place. This is an important point and one I want to emphasise: some people may call it 'commitment', others 'enthusiasm', but *hard work* is also a skill. It is the ability to force yourself to leave your comfort zone and take responsibility for completing tasks to the best of your ability, no matter what else is going on in your life. In this way I could at least be the best I could be.

Hard work often involves long hours and intense focus. From the moment I won my training contract I committed myself to obtaining my accountancy qualification. It was not unusual for me to be in the office from 6.30 in the morning to 9 o'clock at night - a practice that is still common for me today. You may ask where my motivation came from, and the answer is simple: I will never fail because of a lack of application or *hard work* and I do not like losing.

Perhaps stemming from a love of sport, my competitive nature now began to shine through into my work life. The thought of failing my accountancy exams was a great motivation for spurring me on. As a result, at the end of my training contract, out of thirteen colleagues I was one of only three who passed all the exams first time. My drive and *hard work* was not only beginning to pay dividends but was also distinguishing me from my colleagues in the eyes of bosses and clients alike.

My commitment to delivering quality work was fast forming the cornerstone of my reputation. As well as being someone who could communicate with a broad range of people (i.e. be sociable!), I was also beginning to be seen as a safe pair of hands, able to get the job done to a high standard no matter what the situation and with a huge capacity for work even when under pressure (in fact even better under pressure). This latter skill was invaluable, as bosses increasingly gave me more responsibility and interesting cases to deal with. Importantly, I was also starting to really enjoy both the challenge of my job and the recognition that I was quite good at it.

For someone who did not initially find business interesting at university and found the training contract a real challenge, I was now in a position where my core skill of *initiative* - in terms of meeting people and seizing opportunities - allied to my competitive nature, was being acknowledged and rewarded. I found this really satisfying. I want to stress, for those starting out on their careers, that sometimes you need to take on tasks that you do not enjoy as a stepping stone to get to where you want to be. The key is knowing where you want to go. For me, my natural skills of *initiative* and *hard work,* through momentum rather than design, had finally created a platform from which I could shine.

Enjoying my job and the skills I was using I quickly moved up through the grades in the practice to become a manager. Competitors were also noticing my successes. It was therefore not long before an old colleague now working for KPMG asked if I would consider moving with a view to becoming a partner. Still only thirty years of age, I had to pinch myself about how fast my career had developed. Perhaps conditioned by my background and limited academic success, I had never once considered achieving the position of partner as a goal. Nevertheless, the opportunity had now arrived directly as a result of the *initiative* and *hard work* I had demonstrated up to that point. My decision? Well, you know how competitive I am ...!

Interpersonal skills

Being a partner at KPMG is one of the top jobs of my profession. I am routinely involved in steering some of the biggest companies in Scotland through their most difficult trading periods. As such I am seen as a business leader, with my actions and comments widely reported on in the press.

So what is the core skill that can propel aspiring managers to the executive level? For me there is one set that sits above all others, and that is *interpersonal skills*. When reaching the executive level of any business, technical know-how as well as the ability to work hard and seize opportunities are givens; this is equally true of the organisations of my competitors and clients alike. What will distinguish individuals from one another is their interpersonal skills. Interpersonal skills are a mixture of listening, persuading, influencing and negotiating. Put simply, it is about likeability and being able to communicate with others in such a way that they trust and enjoy working with you.

I pride myself in providing an excellent level of service, but there will always be others who have just as good a handle on the latest piece of legislation or can compile reports of a similar standard to mine. Where I excel is in the ability to build relationships with staff and external clients alike on the basis of trust and commitment to excellence; my own personal reputation and proven track record are key elements in this process.

My career development left me ideally placed to maximise the changes that were taking place in my field. For example, up until I secured my training contract both the world of restructuring and insolvency and the senior people within it were dominated by those with strong technical skills. As more competitors entered the market, good technical skills came to be taken for granted and the focus turned increasingly to the selling skills needed to win business. Like us, our main competitors at Deloitte, Ernst & Young and PriceWaterhouseCoopers offered a high level of technical expertise. Our clients understood this. What was winning work for us was our ability to understand clients' needs and express solutions in a manner they could easily understand. As our client list broadened to include a wider array of work providers and their customers, the versatile communication skills I had learned in the sports business allowed me to engage with this emerging marketplace more effectively than many of my peers. This in turn allowed me to win a higher volume of work and work my way up through the company at a far faster rate.

In a short space of time 'Joe Average' was beginning to achieve great success. I came to realise that during your school years you form an opinion about yourself largely based upon your background and what your teachers and friends tell you. The difficulty is that there is no broader context to these judgments. At school you are overwhelmingly judged on your academic ability; the interpersonal skills of listening, adapting your style and conveying your point clearly to others are not assessed. The perception you gain of yourself at school is therefore valuable but limited. For this reason I urge you not to let your educational experience define you. Instead, see schooling as one part of your development. The life experiences you gain through work and social situations are equally important. For once you have a sound bedrock of relevant technical skills, it is your ability to interact well with others that will define how successful you become.

Success in the future marketplace

I have seen a lot of changes during my career. No matter what advances society makes, mastering the core skills of *initiative, hard work,* and *interpersonal skills* will serve any individual well in achieving his or her goals. What I would like to discuss now is the future context in which these skills will be developed. For understanding this context should allow you to broaden your skill set in a more effective manner. To my mind, key themes in the future marketplace will inevitably include the ability to embrace change, the concept of 'work' and the evolving nature of corporate responsibility.

Embracing change

It seems only a short time ago that the business section of a newspaper was the primary means of broadcasting my firm's successes. With the rise of the digital age, and in particular social media, every business leader now has a responsibility to understand how Facebook, Twitter, and LinkedIn (to name but a few) can help show their business in the best light. Central to this is the need to manage reputation, whether it be your own or that of the organisation you represent. It is now commonplace for companies' high profile breaches and misdemeanours to be broadcast across the world within a few minutes, where previously they could be dealt with quietly in-house. With integrity being such a key element of my own business, being able to manage positive perceptions of my work in this environment is becoming increasingly important.

The advent of the digital marketplace has also greatly increased the speed at which things get done. As a leader it is my responsibility to understand how emerging changes can optimise the service we provide clients. To achieve this I do not need to understand how the technology works; I need to build a team that has sufficient knowledge to turn the technology to our advantage. Those who ignore change will inevitably be left behind.

Work/life balance

I have already discussed at some length how hard work has been critical to my success. I am aware though that this concept has changed significantly, in tandem with advances in technology, affecting how we do business. Although I am still the first in the office and the last to leave, I am also sensitive to a new way of working where colleagues can work remotely and have no need to come in. Whilst this is not an approach I would advocate myself - as a manager I prefer to be amongst my colleagues as much as possible - I understand that there is a new generation of employees that increasingly values leisure time over work. For managers like me, who developed their careers in a different generation and work in a highly competitive environment, this can be difficult to deal with.

With the pace of work as it is, and the 24/7 availability of staff thanks to mobile devices, it is right that organisations take on greater responsibility for the wellbeing of their staff. It is important that through relaxation and free personal time staff remain refreshed and up for the challenge. To remain competitive therefore, the business leaders of tomorrow must understand this change and be able to motivate employees by offering relevant incentives and rewards. At KPMG for example, we offer additional holidays, healthcare, and a raft of social pursuits as alternatives to traditional financial incentives. To maintain a motivated staff base committed to service excellence, business leaders must continually listen to their colleagues in order to keep abreast of what remains most important to them.

Corporate social responsibility

The final element of the future marketplace I wish to raise is the increasing role of corporate social responsibility (CSR) in shaping an organisation's reputation.

The world financial crash in 2008, along with a number of high-profile corporate scandals, has rightly given rise to public demand for greater commitment from organisations to their local communities. No longer seen as solely profit-making entities these organisations, or rather their reputation and public perception of them are increasingly being formed by their contributions to the communities they affect.

As chair of KPMG's Corporate Social Responsibility (CSR) committee in our office, this is an obligation that I fully support. KPMG has a long-standing alliance with the charities Shelter and Action for Literacy, and over the last twelve months has been active in many local community projects. In addition to our charity work and fundraising ventures the role of CSR in KPMG also benefits staff, giving them the opportunity to develop transferable skills by working on projects and with people they would not otherwise have encountered. Not least, the positive effect on staff morale of helping others is also greatly rewarding.

When taking on any new client or venture, an organisation increasingly has to acknowledge both the potential effect of its work on its core values and its perceived impact on the local community. Failure to do so will inevitably lead to reputational damage, which will in turn adversely affect client confidence.

Conclusion

The world of business is the world of people. To gain entry to this world you will require a strong foundation in academic learning. This starts at school, with a sound grounding in maths and English. As you specialise in your chosen field – whether you wish to be a hairdresser or lawyer - professional qualifications will demonstrate your understanding to a particular standard. To excel, however, you will need to distinguish yourself from the group. Apply hard work as much to developing your interpersonal skills – how you come across and communicate – as to completing your academic studies. Seek out opportunities to meet new people and do not be afraid of stepping outside your comfort zone. Continually build your own reputation so that you are seen as someone who is trustworthy and can consistently deliver work on time and to a high standard. Above all, be adaptable and ensure that you have some fun along the way!

Chapter 2

The Commonwealth Games Athlete

Jayne Nisbet is a respected international high jumper. Only twenty-five years old, she has represented her country at every level, most notably winning the British Under-23 Championships and British Universities competitions. She has recently been selected to represent Scotland at the 2014 Commonwealth Games sand made it into the High Jump Final. Beyond that, Jayne hopes to represent Great Britain in the 2016 Olympics in Brazil.

Aside from athletics, Jayne has developed her own successful personal training business based in Loughborough. She has also enjoyed success as a model in the fashion industry.

It is Boxing Day. As I compose my thoughts for being interviewed for this book I have just completed my training session for the day. I am also thinking about how best to organise my sessions around my personal training clients for the upcoming week. Being a professional athlete is tiring and there are always pressures upon my time. As I look back on my career I am struck most by the tremendous amount of hard work it is has taken me to get to this point, a factor few outside of athletics can appreciate.

At twenty-five years old, you may be thinking, what can be learned from my story? My reply is that an athlete's career is extremely focused and condenses many of the experiences other individuals learn over a forty-year career. It is certainly not uncommon for people to comment that I am the oldest twenty-five-year-old they have ever met, although I prefer to think it is not the years but the mileage that they are referring to!

For my chapter in this book I want to focus on three skills that I believe are central to being a successful athlete: *persistence, self-management, and courage*. I then go on to discuss the evolving nature of athletics and key themes that I think an aspiring athlete should consider in order to achieve success. Before covering these areas in detail, I want to start with what inspired me to become an athlete in the first place.

A competitive edge

I have always had an interest in athletics. This was undoubtedly helped by my family background, as both my parents have always been keen on sports and encouraged me to be the same. The real inspiration, however, was my brother. Being the youngest (and smallest) in the family I was always trying to be noticed and match my sporty brother. To this end I played football, golf and hockey, and swam at national level when in my teens. My early passion for sport soon turned into success, as I regularly won the school sports day at high school. It is important to note, however, that while talented I was never tipped as a future star. Nor did I really care. I just loved the thrill of competing and knew that in sport I had found something I was keen to pursue.

At school I was tall for my age (I am 5'8") and I was always being encouraged by my sports coaches through school to try for the high jump. I had some early success by being the best in my school and coming second at the British Athletic Association (BAA) youth games when only fifteen years old. It was through this experience that I began to focus on high jump, triple jump, and long jump.

Between the ages of sixteen and twenty-one I had a really good coach and benefited from his guidance. During this period I represented Great Britain at the European Junior Championships, won the Under-23 British Championships and then the British Universities Championships. My success in these competitions proved a real turning point. I now believed that with commitment and hard work I could really compete at the top level.

Faced with the prospect of leaving school and pursuing a career or attending university, I knew I was at a crossroads in both my professional and personal development (because you can never really separate the two). As I was enjoying working with my coach I decided to attend Stirling University because this would allow us to train together. Although it involved commuting daily from my home in Edinburgh – and missing out on the university experience of living in halls – I understood from an early age that this commitment to my training, allied with a consistent coach, would pay dividends later in my career.

Skills for success

Persistence
At this point in my story I wish to discuss the first main skill that I believe is crucial to being a successful athlete - *persistence*. To me, *persistence* is the ability to keep moving forward to your goal no matter what obstacles are placed in your way. From my own experience of competing, and being based at the centre of sporting excellence at Loughborough University, I am constantly in the presence of elite athletes. For those not involved in sport it is easy to assume that world-class athletes such as Jessica Ennis or Usain Bolt are simply born that way. It is not true. Every athlete I know has had to overcome rejection and challenges in their life to achieve the success they enjoy today.

My journey was no different. From one perspective, by the age of twenty-one my career trajectory was following the right direction: I was achieving success in most competitions I entered; I was performing well at university; and I was building a reputation as a rising star. In any walk of life, however, you cannot separate the professional performance from the personal life of the individual - a lesson I was soon to learn.

Becoming an elite athlete is as much about off-field management as it is about on-field performance. Primarily, the realm of sports nutrition and science has taken on increasing importance in athletics over the past generation. From the age of seventeen I was exposed to the concept of sports nutrition as a precursor to boosting my on-field performance. Although I was committed to my sport and understood that I had to look after my diet, it was sometimes difficult to maintain my discipline when those of the same age around me were attending parties and eating what they wanted.

Perhaps it was the intensity of competing at a level where the slightest change in diet can give you an advantage. Or perhaps it was the part-time modelling work I undertook and the emphasis on my physical appearance that came with it. Whatever the reason, and unknown to me for a number of years, between the ages of eighteen and twenty-four I developed the eating disorders of anorexia and bulimia. For those who do not know, anorexia is an eating disorder of excessive weight loss. Bulimia is characterised by binge eating in a short period of time followed by an attempt to rid oneself of the food such as by being sick. Whatever the cause, these conditions were increasingly affecting my performance during the formative years of my career.

You may be wondering why my coaches or those close to me failed to recognise the symptoms. Because elite athletes are 'super fit' it is perhaps more difficult to spot these conditions in them than in other people. As a result of constant training it is not abnormal for a professional athlete's body fat to be around three per cent.

The eating disorders were beginning to have a real impact on my performance. It was not uncommon for me to be unable to walk following training. Some days I could not even function past breakfast. My mood also varied wildly. I visited my doctor and was prescribed anti-depressants, but they only increased my feelings of emptiness. I no longer had the same buzz. As a result I failed to qualify for the 2010 Commonwealth Games in Delhi – a competition I had been tipped to do well in never mind qualify for.

I had hit rock bottom. At this point I seriously wondered whether I could achieve success at the elite level. I had worked for years to qualify for Delhi. The fact that I not only failed to do so but was also feeling so bad after training inevitably caused me to question whether all the effort was worth it. At this point I remember a particular conversation I had with my coach. He simply asked me who I thought was 'driving [my]bus', and told me to be sure that everyone on that bus was 'helping [me] towards my destination.' This conversation was like a light bulb going on inside my head. I suddenly realised that I was unhappy in my personal life and that this unhappiness was manifesting in my poor performance on the field.

I therefore resolved to make wholesale changes in my life and create a more positive atmosphere around me. I ended a poor relationship and refocused. I attended sessions with a psychotherapist who allowed me to understand the trigger events in my life – such as the pressure of upcoming tournaments – and devise coping mechanisms to help manage those situations better. I also changed my coach. Most importantly, I set myself the goal of qualifying for the 2014 Commonwealth Games to inspire me to work through all the obstacles in my way.

Moving into 2012 the obstacles still came. I suffered a freak injury which delayed my winter training camp - a crucial period for any athlete and for me more so with Commonwealth qualifiers being held in early 2013. I was different now, though. I had my freshness back because I now understood the areas in my life that could give rise to poor performance and was able to manage them in a much more proactive and positive way. I was back competing with a smile on my face.

I opened the 2013 season with a third place finish at the British Championships, which was a solid achievement considering my injury in late 2012. A week later I competed at the Scottish Indoor Championships and won. As the season progressed I worked through the Commonwealth qualifiers and finally won my place.

When I walk out in the opening ceremony at Hampden Park in August 2014 in many ways it will be an achievement in itself and a symbol of my *persistence* in achieving my goal in the face of significant personal challenges. Without the focus of the Commonwealth Games it is likely that I would have been sitting on a couch watching the event rather than competing in it. The story of overcoming adversity is true for every athlete, only the circumstances are different. Others may be told they are too fat, too short, or too slow. What allows them to move past these criticisms is their unshakeable belief that they will succeed because their *persistence* is fortified by a clearly defined goal.

Self-management

My goal of qualifying for the 2014 Commonwealth Games motivated me to persist and rise above the obstacles in my way. It is important to mention that the only person who could make that dream a reality was me. Though supported by a loving family and a team of skilled coaches, I was the one above all others who had to apply the hard work to make success happen. Thus, the athlete must also possess a great deal of *self-management*.

Although I am a professional athlete, I still do not receive enough financial assistance through the sport for me to concentrate full-time on my training. I need to have a job like everyone else. Being a personal trainer I do have the benefit of being able to organise my client commitments around my training sessions. I train six days a week, with double training sessions every second day. It is therefore not uncommon for me to be up at 5.00am, have my first client at 6.00am, then start my own training later that day with another session in the evening. Yes, it can be very tiring and so self-management is the key and pervades all areas of my life. For example, as well as organising my training and business commitments, I also need to pay great attention to my diet and resting periods.

As you may gather, such commitment also has an impact on my personal life. Through experience I have learned the importance of taking a balanced approach to my career. In such an intense and focused profession it is easy to become consumed by the competitive nature of the sport. To keep things in perspective it is crucial to have time away from the track with family and loved ones. This is also key to maintaining a fresh mental edge.

During the period of managing my eating disorders I felt I had lost my spark. Competing became routine and I no longer had any buzz. By making changes in my personal and professional life – essentially removing areas of negativity – my self-motivation increased. I had more energy. I began to feel good about myself. This positivity translated into my on-field performance, with people observing that I was smiling much more. I could not wait to get out there!

So what keeps me motivated to maintain such a level of dedication? Primarily, simply a love of the sport and competing. You will find in any sport that competitors are in it either for the game or for the fame; those in the latter camp do not tend to reach elite level. I love high jumping. I want to be the best I can be. To do this I understand that I need rivals of the same level to push me to the limit of my potential. I am therefore not motivated by failure but by the positive effects competition can have on my own performance level. I welcome the competition.

Courage

The final skill I wish to discuss on my road to success is *courage*. What I mean by this term is perhaps best summed up by my coach, who said: '*do not let the fear of striking out stop you playing the game!*' To achieve success in any field – never mind athletics – you need to challenge your own comfort zones. To achieve an elite level of performance I have been aided greatly by the support and guidance of my coaches and loved ones. Listening is one thing, however; the courage to take advice then commit to change is more difficult.

From my own journey the best example of my courage is how I challenged my eating disorders. I realised that there was a problem and I sought help. More importantly, I made changes to the routines in my life – both mental and physical – that were causing me harm. Gaining that level of courage requires you to be honest with yourself. Ultimately you are the only person who can help yourself. Achieving that level of honesty can be very difficult, but I was inspired to change my behaviour by identifying the benefits it would bring me - better on-field performance and, most importantly, feeling better about myself.

Courage requires motivation too. I have taken this concept and applied it to all areas of my life. When improving my technique during training, it can be difficult and frustrating to change something I have done for years. By understanding the improvement to my performance it will bring about, the change becomes slightly easier to make.

I have also demonstrated courage in my working life. Never the most academic at school, I found gaining my personal training qualifications challenging. Furthermore, the emphasis on my training from a young age restricted my ability to socialise when at high school. As a result I have always been more shy than outgoing. Being a personal trainer, with its emphasis on meeting and advising so many different people, really pushed me out of my comfort zone. I am pleased to say, though, that like my athletic career my personal training business has been a great success. When faced with a difficult situation I now have the experience of combating my eating disorders, running my own business, and achieving a place at the Commonwealth Games to prove to myself that I can make positive changes in my life. This confidence has inevitably helped me develop both as an athlete and as a person.

The athletic career is a short one, and thus every athlete is under pressure to peak at the big events. Negative thoughts of under-performing or picking up an injury can weigh heavily for some and inhibit their ability to push themselves on. I have experienced both the pain of injury and the disappointment of missing a big event. I keep my mental frame by not over-analysing situations. I keep it simple. I know that by continually doing the right things and having the right habits I will reduce the chance of injury and raise my performance level. The spectre of disappointment is always there, but I now choose to have the courage to move beyond it and concentrate on the feeling of enjoying the competition and being the best athlete I can be.

Future developments

Diet

The analysis of athletic performance is becoming increasingly scientific. This can best be seen in the area of sports nutrition. In my own career, I am very particular about what and when I eat, because I know that at the elite level it could ultimately make the difference between winning and not winning a medal.

The testing and scrutiny of athletes for taking banned substances has also increased. High-profile examples such as the Lance Armstrong case are proof that such practices remain prevalent across sport. It is important to make the distinction, however, between those who wilfully take a banned substance and those who fail testing through their own ignorance. In my own experience it is not uncommon to hear of athletes failing tests through taking items such as cough medicines that can be bought without prescription. Any aspiring athlete, and especially those operating at the elite level, should take responsibility for educating themselves about permitted substances. Everyone, no matter what their job, has to work within certain rules, policies and procedures and so it is important that everyone - even athletes - are familiar with them. There are websites to assist athletes in identifying banned substances and it is up to individuals to be aware of their responsibilities in this regard.

On a more positive note, the correct management of sports nutrition can really enhance an athlete's level of performance. I would advise any person new to the sport to read up on sports nutrition and be honest about how their current diet could be improved. Knowledge of rest periods, sleep patterns and optimum training periods can also be of great benefit.

Essentially you should be able to reach a point when you know you have put your body and mind in an optimum position for performance.

Reputation-building

In the build up to the Commonwealth Games I am aware that my public profile will increase. This is especially true because I will be representing the host country. At the time of contributing to this chapter I am unsure how this media interest will manifest. I hope it will be positive and will come about as a result of me winning a medal!

From the 2012 Olympics we have seen individuals such as Jessica Ennis rise through their achievements to become household names and almost brands in their own right. Whilst it would be a privilege to share in such success, I am also experienced enough to know that such attention has to be managed correctly. We are all aware that through social media such as Facebook and Twitter many prominent individuals have posted comments or pictures - often before they achieved public prominence - that have since come back to haunt them.

In all the excitement in the lead-up to the 2014 Commonwealth Games it will be a challenge to maintain my focus. The media attention will therefore be another potential distraction. To manage this correctly I would simply advise any aspiring athlete to use their common sense when it comes to managing their public reputation. When making any comment or posting any picture just be mindful of what message you may be conveying, especially to people who do not know you. Whilst it is great to have the support of the public, on the flip side no athlete wants to have to manage comments about their personal life while preparing for the most important event of their life.

Conclusion

Athletics is something I love. I enjoy competing and the challenge of trying to improve my performance each time I take to the track. For some athletes, when their hobby becomes their profession they can lose that buzz of simply wanting to be their best. The personal sacrifices you must make and the pressure of managing your own and others' expectations of your performance can weigh heavily on you. By reading about my journey you have seen my own personal challenges in dealing with eating disorders and the disappointment of missing major events.

My participation in the 2014 Commonwealth Games was never a given. I won my place through *persistence* to achieve my goal. Every athlete there will have a similar story. The point is that elite performers are formed through their handling of setbacks. They continually demonstrate the *courage* to continue. This courage is fuelled not just by a belief in their ability, but most importantly by a love of what they do and the buzz they get from being pushed by other like-minded individuals to the peak of their ability.

I would advise any aspiring athletes to find the discipline in which they have the most fun. That way the ability to motivate themselves to train and make sacrifices comes that bit easier. To supplement the advice given by coaches, each athlete should take responsibility for educating themselves in their chosen sport. Each day of training is about not only building your level of performance but also forming a perception of yourself. Make sure the reputation you develop is based on hard work, honesty, and commitment; people will then be more likely to help you along your way!

Chapter 3
The Chef and Restaurant Owner

Craig Wilson is a chef with a worldwide reputation. He was one of the youngest head chefs in the country and also one of the youngest chefs to achieve two AA rosettes for his culinary skills. He has cooked for well-known figures such as Sir Sean Connery, Patrick Stewart, Alex Salmond MSP and Sir Alex Ferguson.

Whilst appearing in the final of TV cookery challenge, 'Pot Idol', the host Lorraine Kelly affectionately called Craig the Kilted Chef. The name stuck and Craig's reputation has continued to grow as a result of his hard work, skill and artistic flair. His skill for using everyday ingredients to create a range of different dishes has earned him international acclaim. Craig is also director of his own restaurant, 'Eat on the Green', in the North East of Scotland. His passion for food and using only the best local ingredients also helped him to clinch a win for Scotland in a culinary Six Nations Tournament on the Irish television programme, The Afternoon Show. Going head to head with one of Ireland's Michelin starred chefs, Craig brought home the title.

I was born and bred in the north east of Scotland. In my school days I did not feel that I fitted in. I struggled a bit and looking back I probably needed more support. I was written off by a primary teacher and again in secondary school by my home economics teacher! If I had had a different teacher I might have been encouraged more.

My passion for food began at an early age. I was lucky I connected with something that was and still is my passion. As a young boy I wanted to become a butcher. I remember my mother taking me to the two butchers' shops in the village and the impression their sights and smells made on me. I think I was attracted to working in a butcher's by the practical side of things. My grandmother also encouraged my very early involvement in food: not just food, but good food. My mother cooked because she had to, but my grandfather was a gardener and my grandmother cooked some fine foods sourced locally. Hence my passion for good food and local produce was ignited. Some people work with food but have no relationship with it. They do not understand it and so become very robotic. I always understood and respected where food came from, and this made working with good food very easy for me.

In secondary school I did okay but I was a like a caged animal. I knew what I wanted to do and could not wait to get out. I had four part-time jobs, all at the same time. I had two paper rounds, a job in a grocery store, and then once I finished them I jumped on a bus and went off to wash dishes. I was maybe a bit greedy but the experience taught me good lessons about hard work and determination. I soon learned that if you do a good job you get rewarded and recognised. I remember an older lady working in a restaurant being unhappy with the work I was putting in and being clearly jealous. She even locked me in a cupboard at one point. Later that evening she slipped on the floor and became lodged under the sink- I believe very strongly in karma! Thus I also learned quickly that not everyone has the same drive as me, but that if I worked hard and found solutions to work challenges then I would get on.

At the age of sixteen I started out as a trainee chef at the Strathburn Hotel in Inverurie and I also attended day release at college. This was a great starting point for an ambitious young man, but I realised early in life that I would need to move to achieve success. Leaving my rural roots behind then, I moved south to Perthshire to work at Ballathie House Hotel. It meant taking a fifty per cent pay cut but it was worth it. I had to start again. I had to learn new things, meet new people and develop myself. It was one of the most exciting things I had ever done.

At this point I just wanted to conquer the world, I had so much determination. With my next move - a major promotion to head chef at one of the finest luxury hotels in Scotland, Cromlix House - I came one step closer to achieving my goals. I had earned this promotion not necessarily because I was the best but because I worked hard, and was determined and conscientious. At only twenty-four years of age I was now one of the youngest head chefs in the country. More success was to come when I became one of the youngest chefs to be awarded two AA rosettes. Even with all this success I knew I could never afford to be complacent and had to keep working hard. Cooking is so personal – not everyone likes everything so I constantly needed to improve, evaluate and learn what pleased the majority of my customers

After three years at Cromlix House I took on a different role in new product development with Grampian Country Foods, before heading to Grimsby to continue my development chef role with Baxters Food Group. There was nobody prouder. There was an element of 'royalty' that came with working for such a big brand and I just loved it. There were parts of it that were not romantic, but I knew I was working with one of the big players. I loved the story of a family man making jars of jam in the shop which he had borrowed money to open. From this humble beginning in Fochabers in Scotland, Baxters went on to become a major supermarket brand.

My placement there was supposed to last for six months but ended up lasting almost a year. It was a year that changed me. The company developed people, which I respected and embraced, and treated them well. I was out of the hotel and restaurant environment and now researching new trends in food. My job was a chef's dream: thinking up new ideas with no financial constraints. It was amazing to think that very quickly a new concept we were working with could be on the shop shelves. I also spent a lot of time in London, which was a major culture shock for a boy from the north east of Scotland. The experience served me very well and was mightily exciting. I learned to negotiate and encourage people, and how to share my passion with others in a more business-like style. I also expanded the network of people I knew. Later in life I was to work with a marketing company I had met in London during that time.

Moving away and having new experiences has been a major influence on me and where I am now. In London I dreamed of having a restaurant and even sketched out what its front door might look like. I wanted it to look like Number 10 Downing Street: a clean, black, painted door with a shiny handle and letter box. It is amazing to think that all these years later I had the opportunity to return there last month. The green sign that adorns the front of my restaurant today was inspired by the green of Harrods because I wanted to replicate something of my experience in London. We are all products of our environments. It is great to get out there and experience as much as you can early in life.

After all my travelling and the experience I gained, I was inspired to do it for myself. Having worked hard, and with a bit of luck from the property boom, I managed to generate enough equity to realise my dream of owning a place I could call my own. I took the plunge and opened my own restaurant serving high quality food using the finest local ingredients. To do this I returned to my roots, the north east of Scotland. 'Eat on the Green' was born.

It is amazing to think what has happened since I first thought of owning my own restaurant. Resting on the idyllic village green of quaint Udny Green, Eat on the Green was once a small, dilapidated, village pub. Now it is a high-quality, fine-dining restaurant that has become known as one of the best restaurants in the north east of Scotland, securing numerous accolades since it opened.

Skills for success

I could not have earned some of those accolades without a number of key skills that have been vital throughout my career and which remain so. *Teamwork* is so important, but so too is having *stamina and determination*, setting *high standards* and being able to give something else back. In such a busy workplace you need to think about what makes you feel good and what makes you healthy and well. Giving something back is an act we all want to do regularly but just need to make the time to do it.

Teamwork

I started off as a one-man band, but as the restaurant has grown so has my team. *Teamwork* has been a vital ingredient of our success. I now have five full time chefs and a team of thirty people. One of the most important elements in the success of the restaurant has been that every member of staff is important to me and each one understands how crucial their role is. Each member of the team is vital to delivering our aim of a 'five-star customer experience.'

Investing in people and teamwork is so important in any work environment and I really try to invest in my staff. I am so fortunate to be supported by a dedicated, conscientious and talented team that consistently delivers on my high standards of food and service. However, it needs to be worked at continually! *Teamwork* does not come naturally and is a skill that is developed through time. Nor is it always plain sailing even then. Sometimes people let you down or do not do things to the standard everyone expects. When this happens, I have learned through time, it is best to say something constructive and then praise the work when it is carried out properly.

During recruitment interviews, as well as explaining to potential employees the different roles in the restaurant we explain a lot about our ethos too. We are one team. For example, we have started to rotate roles in the team. A chef with seven years' experience is now working with us and will be spending part of his time working with the front of house staff who take the orders from customers. Not only is the experience of customer contact itself valuable, but performing the roles of other teams more generally helps staff to find ways of working better together by understanding other people's pressures and challenges.

Teams do, however, need a strong leader, and they need to be orderely. In my kitchen and restaurant I have everything where I want it. It is my cockpit. Every night there is a chance of turbulence so I need to know where everything is and what everything can do so that we can work through any problems- without the customer being aware. As I said earlier, if you are not happy with something in the team you need to say so. If you do not tackle the small things early on then they snowball and can do a lot of damage to the whole product. People need to receive encouragement and be rewarded for good performance, but leaders also need to be clear when things are not going right.

I was not always keen to be so honest. If you care for your product, your service and/or your reputation, though, then in a team setting you must take action. Your reputation means something to you personally. If something is not right you tend to know it is not right, and if you do not know, your customers will tell you. It is so important that you take action to put things right. Nothing happens by accident. Some people have their own agenda. which makes things more difficult - it is so important to have a shared vision of what you are trying to achieve. Once everyone in the team has the same goals and vision it becomes like a well oiled machine. In such a team every individual counts.

Stamina and perseverance

Anyone entering the restaurant trade needs to be aware that it is hard work. It can look easy when you watch celebrity chefs on TV or see well-trained and highly skilled chefs working in restaurants. But the reality is that it requires a lot of hard work, *stamina* and *perseverance*. Weekends spent working in a restaurant can be like a long-haul flight - at the end of it you are completely shattered, but hopefully proud of your efforts. You can go from helping to prepare food for a wedding to catering for a funeral, from a romantic meal for two to a a large party of corporate guests. Each one expects and deserves the same high standard. The only way to achieve this is by putting the same effort into each and every job that you do. It is hard work but it pays off.

Attention to detail and maintaining consistently high standards

I pride myself and my staff on maintaining a five-star standard. To do that I need to do certain things. Perseverance plays a part, as does teamwork, but I also work on the theory that I must lead by example, and when it comes to maintaining standards *attention to detail* is what counts. It applies to the smallest things and is vitally important. So, if we say we are going to polish the front door twice a day then we must do just that. We must make sure that we do it every day, twice a day. If we keep to that *high standard* then it becomes part of us.

I said earlier that teamwork is the biggest challenge in the hospitality business, but individual standards make up the various parts of that team. There are so many variables when you are working with people. How someone looks, smells and sounds can make an instant impression on people - are they encouraged, discouraged, encouraging or discouraging? There are days when you do not feel or look great, but you must always put on a show for your customers. You cannot cover everything up because you need to be honest. But you need to be the best you can be even when you are not feeling one hundred per cent. To do that your teams must be motivated, as a unit and individually. I often ask members of the team how they think they are viewed by others because the question encourages useful self-evaluation. Everyone has to maintain a high standard. Above all, people who work in this trade must be bona fide people-pleasers, with an innate desire to please. If you are not in this category – look for a job elsewhere!

Future considerations

Looking ahead to the future, there are a number of key skills that I think will be important in the food and drink industry, which each new entrant should consider. Maintaining high standards will always be crucial. However, whilst it is all very well having a trophy cabinet, it needs to be constantly polished and refreshed.

Developing a sixth sense

A restaurant becomes an extension of what you are and who you are. I can walk into the restaurant and just sense when things are going well or when there is a problem. You develop a feel for it. I do not just want to get by. I want to do the best I can, and knowing when things are going well or not is therefore really important. Some of that ability comes from establishing a formula that works. It is so important to get into good habits because habit-forming is, I believe, a key ingredient of success.

Another example of where a sixth sense will help you can be seen from an occasion when one of my chefs asked me about ingredient weights for a new dish we were preparing. He wanted me to tell him the exact weights to apply, but the reality is that it will vary according to what is right for different customers at different times. For example, some people might just have a main course whilst others might have a full three-course meal. Alternatively I might be serving a hungry businesswoman who wants a good but light lunch and then a sixty-year-old man who is in for a longer and more substantial evening meal. Hence the need also to be flexible.

Finally under this heading, I remember a time when we had a power cut during the day. Everyone thought we should close the restaurant that night, but I just knew that we had to open. I sent a message round all staff telling them to prepare themselves for the fact that we would be opening. We did open- with camping stoves and candles at the ready. Thanks to my warning everyone was primed and ready to deliver a five-star service again. The power did come back on but we had everything in place to cope had it not and I had a good sense of what was required to lead the team to ensure first class service was maintained.

Giving something back

A key skill for the future is having the values and ability to give something back. For me it is a vital skill for anyone who is successful. It always amazes me how strongly committed young people are to helping others. We tend to lose that attitude as we get older and busier, but we should hold on to it. I am deeply passionate about charity work. When I think deeper about what motivates me I ask myself this: 'What makes me happy?' Sometimes asking the question is more powerful than the answer itself.

Despite long hours grafting in the kitchen, I am very committed to fundraising for cancer charities. Our efforts have been successful, raising well over £100k over the last six years, and we continue to raise more. I also support the local community with donations to schools, playgroups and smaller charitable organisations. All these organisations need support and I receive around ten letters a week looking for help. I do what I can not only to raise funds for these very worthy causes but also, where I can, to raise a charity's profile. It is great when we can do that by involving the community and creating a 'feel good' factor for all those involved. I have been really fortunate that the success of my business has allowed me to work with charities that are closest to my heart.

In 2008, hundreds of people enjoyed a 'Food & Fun Day' on our village green, raising £13k for Breast Cancer Care. In the same year, for the same cause we raised another £10k with a 24-hour cookathon, serving over three hundred covers throughout the day and night without sleeping. Not only was this a lot of fun, we raised a huge amount for charity and felt great during the process. Then in 2011 I embarked on my biggest challenge yet, cooking in every Scottish city in just one day. With the aid of a helicopter donated by local businessman and great friend Bryan Keith, a massive network of supporters and months of planning, I travelled six hundred miles to cook in Inverness, Aberdeen, Dundee, Stirling, Edinburgh and Glasgow, before returning to Udny Green for the finale. This charity challenge alone raised over £30k in support of the new Maggie's Cancer Caring Centre in Aberdeen and Breast Cancer Care.

Determination

We all know that it is not easy to succeed in business, and even harder during a global recession. Although we are now in a strong position, we did not escape unscathed. We were fortunate that our strategy and niche as a special occasion restaurant in the fine-dining sector, together with a robust local economy, meant that our customers still celebrated their birthdays and anniversaries etc. with us even though they dined out less overall. We are beyond thankful that our restaurant and its reputation were well established prior to the recession, because our location means we cannot rely on passing trade. Our unwavering attention to detail and determination not to accept any reduction in standards both front and back of house are the pillars of strength that have kept our doors from closing.

Our rise from gastropub to fine-dining restaurant has not been easy. The additional staff costs and equipment associated with this level of service meant a huge rise in operating costs. Nevertheless, we knew we had the foundations of a strong business, our turnover was still increasing year on year and we were not prepared to fail.

Having worked hard to get the business into a healthy state we have not stood still since. In 2012, we invested in a new showpiece Chef's Table adjoining the kitchen. This comfortable and stylish room contains a live TV link to the hot plate, offering our customers a unique, private dining experience. Now guests pay a surcharge to hire this room, which is popular for private business meetings and with high profile guests.

Eager to keep ahead of our competition in the city and always daring to be different, in the summer of 2013, we launched Scotland's first Laurent-Perrier Champagne Members Lounge, *Le Salon Vert'*. This has added a world-class touch to our establishment. Following our successful pitch to the Champagne house, Laurent-Perrier shared fifty per cent of the costs of building, furnishing and promoting our stunning new garden room. Membership is based upon an annual fee and advance purchase of cellar stock for use throughout the year. The income generated from this exclusive club covered our investment. With a waiting list for new members, we can be confident of its continued success.

Bizarrely we are grateful for the recession, as it allowed our business to focus and flourish whilst many other establishments with lower standards closed. This year we plan to become a 'restaurant with rooms' to capitalise on that particular market opportunity, to expand further into premium outside catering - for which we have already established a demand - and to re-model our kitchen areas to facilitate this growth.

Health and wellbeing
I am a passionate believer in the importance of having good health and wellbeing. Securing this can be difficult at times, but can be accomplished by taking some simple steps.

It is essential to have the right mental mindset. I think as a youngster it is vital that you surround yourself with the right, positive-minded people, such as being part of a team, a family or a group that is supportive and inspirational to you. In your youth you have a lovely blank canvas; take the opportunity to paint something on it that is bright, positive and what you want it to be. It is so important to aspire to achieve.

I am also a passionate believer in the positive impact that good food can have on our physical and mental wellbeing. I have been doing a lot of work looking at the benefits of eating good food at difficult times, particularly amongst cancer sufferers. Patients can take great strength and joy from good food. When you are diagnosed with cancer you go right back to basics. Pure and simple foods are great for the body and the mind. At all ages in your life, a little more understanding of the right food and drink for your body is so powerful. When your body is being challenged why not give it its very best chance by feeding it well. It is very easy to forget, or get side-tracked or not give it enough time but you should make time and get into the habit of eating well at regular times. Seasonal, fresh foods are so important to me and I believe that others should give them more consideration too. They look better, smell better and make you feel better, and when you feel better you have a better chance of success. I work closely with local schools/clubs, and also now the Rowett Institute of Nutrition and Health, to spread the word about health and happy eating.

I have already mentioned the benefits of habit forming in establishing good working practices, but it is also conducive to good health and wellbeing. I have a personal trainer, which helps me to establish that particular habit. Just as in the workplace, if you have said you will do something twice times a day then you must stick to it. Once you stop it is hard to get back into it, but if you adopt it as a habitual part of your life then you will not use up energy unnecessarily worrying about getting round to it. I try to keep a good balance between enjoying myself and maintaining a good weight. Food is a passion but also a demon. I know that if I have too much I am not happy in myself. I know when I am not at one hundred per cent: not only do I not feel well on the inside but the same is true of the outside.

Conclusion

Overall, what would be my key skills for success? Well I have mentioned a few above but the one that keeps on coming through as being vital, is getting into good habits. Habit forming starts with a regular good breakfast and goes right through to the way in which you work and relate to others. Developing the right habits will lead to success if it is combined with determination, attention for detail, passion for what you do and the appetite to achieve.

Habits, health and happiness - that would about best sum it up. If there were more happier and healthier people in the world it would be a far better place.

Chapter 4

The Life Scientist

Nicola Stanley-Wall is a reader in microbiology and deputy head of the Division of Molecular Microbiology at the University of Dundee. She received her PhD from the University of East Anglia in 2000 and was an EMBO (European Molecular Biology Organisation) long-term fellow at the University of California in Los Angeles from 2001 to 2005. After being awarded a BBSRC (Biotechnology and Biological Sciences Research Council) David Phillips Fellowship she moved to the College of Life Sciences at the University of Dundee to establish her own research team.

Nicola is interested in how single-celled bacteria can act at as a multicellular community to inhabit and exploit their environment. She uses a range of molecular biology techniques alongside mathematical modelling and high-powered microscopy to conduct her research. She is interested in science communication and is currently a BBSRC School Regional Champion.

My job is to investigate how bacteria come together to form social communities (called 'biofilms'). The greater understanding we have of this process, the more effective we can be in combating harmful bacterial infections. I love my job as it involves original thinking, scientific enquiry, and versatility: skills that I have enjoyed developing over the course of my career. The fact that I use these skills in the field of biology – an area in which I have always had a real interest – greatly adds to my feeling of job satisfaction.

My current role as reader in microbiology and deputy head of the Division of Molecular Microbiology at the University of Dundee is very specialised. I therefore wish to use this article to explore my career choices and discuss the skills that have been central to my development. I shall conclude my discussion by exploring the future trends in my profession and the skills required to meet emerging challenges.

My journey

Looking back I feel extremely fortunate that from a young age my 'education' extended beyond the classroom and included real life situations. This largely resulted from my own initiative, as I began volunteering from the age of fourteen in a local country park. Working on conservation projects, my work was a natural fit as I always had an interest in natural history and nature. My duties were broad and included digging ditches, putting up fences and acting as a helper when showing young children around the park. I really enjoyed being outside and learning about nature.

During that period I also volunteered as a carer for the elderly. Achieving bronze, silver, and gold Duke of Edinburgh awards my volunteering was invaluable as it increased my confidence and self-esteem, and helped sharpen my focus on potential future careers. Not only that, I learned the key skills of being able to get along well with a broad range of people, compassion and taking responsibility for my actions.

In sum, I believe that my volunteering experience allowed me to mature faster than my peers. I had been exposed to real life and gained the confidence to know that I could meet life's challenges head on. As such, I would urge any young person to become involved in the Duke of Edinburgh scheme or volunteer for local community projects. In addition, part of my growing independence was dependent on my self-management skills. As you can imagine, volunteering placed significant demands on my time. During that period I also had to maintain a responsibility to my studies and social life. I was a good student and found that my volunteering was a good way to keep a fresh perspective on life. More specifically, my experience helped me to form a clear idea of the careers I would enjoy pursuing.

Identifying a career path

I really enjoyed my volunteering experience of caring for the elderly. I found helping others very rewarding. Before I left school I became keen on nursing as a potential career. My parents knew my interests well, however, and suggested that a career involving biology might be better suited to my interests.

Biology was always one of my favourite subjects. My school work included classes on DNA and molecular biology; these were areas that I found really interesting. Moving through school I pursued this interest and studied molecular biology in my sixth year. I felt as though I had discovered hidden secrets of how the world around us was made. It was really exciting. The approaches used in molecular biology also suited how I learned, with their stress on step-by-step procedures and strong emphasis on fact-based conclusions. I found the exactness and logical procedures a natural fit with how my mind worked. Based on what I enjoyed doing, I enrolled in a three-year degree course in biological sciences at the University of East Anglia.

University life

The confidence and independence I had gained through volunteering prepared me well for the challenges of settling into university life. This is quite an important point, as I believe every experience furnishes you with a lesson or skill that can help prepare you for future challenges. Throughout my career I have seen how some find it hard to move away from home, adapt well to new surroundings or make new friends. Through my volunteering work I had quickly learned how to find common interests with others, which is essentially the basis for forming friendships. From my Duke of Edinburgh experience I had spent time away from home before, so the move to university was less daunting for me than for others.

The most enjoyable aspect of my degree came in my third year when I had the opportunity to work full time for a bio-technology company in Cambridge. Organised as part of my course, the objective was to provide students with vocational experience of applying their academic learning in a practical, corporate environment - another formative experience for me. To win a place I had to apply through a formal process and pass an interview. Upon being successful, I then had to move away (again). As a result of financial constraints I lived in a YMCA for six months while I worked for the company. Whilst I found this initially daunting, the experience I had already gained in meeting new people allowed me to settle in quickly both to my new living arrangements and working life. The daily work in the lab validated my decision to pursue a career in research science. I enjoyed the precise nature of the work and being part of a close-knit team.

Following my placement I returned to university to complete my degree. I obtained the highest grade and decided to study for my PhD, which would allow me to specialise further. My decision to commit to further study was largely based on the fact that I enjoyed what I was doing. PhD work provided me with more time to work in the lab. I was beginning to direct my own work and start exploring areas that were of real interest to me. I found this exciting. I came to have my work published and had the opportunity to attend conferences and seminars with other like-minded people, an experience I found richly rewarding.

Studying for a PhD is incredibly demanding. You need to be extremely conscious of your self-management because time always seems to be in short supply. You also require emotional resilience as your work becomes routinely scrutinised by your peers. I have encountered some students who find this experience uncomfortable because they do not respond well to criticism. Whilst no-one enjoys being told they are wrong, I have always viewed criticism as being central to my development as a professional. It is only through people challenging my work that I can improve my approach and develop my working practices to a higher level, thereby producing a higher quality of work. Now that I am in a position to offer guidance to PhD students I am always mindful of this when delivering my critiques of others' work in this context.

A new start

As happens with many students, I met my husband whilst we were studying the same course. He finished his doctoral work at the same time as I did. The opportunity then arose for me to continue my research work at the University of California in Los Angeles. This was an exciting and a scary challenge in equal measure! It was also an opportunity I knew would enrich me both socially and professionally, so I grabbed it with both hands.

Los Angeles is much like you may have seen on television: really hot, really big and ethnically diverse! Living in Hollywood was the first time in my life I considered myself to be in a minority, as my neighbourhood was predominantly Hispanic. I approached this situation much like I did my volunteering, university life, and living in the YMCA - with an open mind. I quickly made friends and really enjoyed the opportunity of working in another country, and outside of working in the lab I travelled extensively and really felt broadened as a person.

My experience in Los Angeles also demonstrated that the life of a scientist is often short term and fleeting. I saw many colleagues come and go, because due to budget constraints contracts were often short term. Now married, I decided a more permanent role would best suit my personal circumstances. When I was offered a job as lecturer in microbiology at the University of Dundee, it was an opportunity that excited me because again it seemed a natural fit. As well as giving me job security, the university also had a great reputation in my field and offered superb research facilities.

My current role

Now a reader, my job involves the same variety of skills that has characterised my career since I began volunteering as a fourteen-year old, with the common theme of biology running throughout. I am still a research scientist, and a great deal of my time is spent investigating inside the lab. I have also developed business acumen through having to apply for financial support to fund the various projects in which I am involved.

My role as mentor for PhD students is also rewarding, as I help them through the same process and learning I went through only ten years before. Beyond the university environment, I have also maintained my commitment to the local community. I have instigated public engagement work with Dundee Science Centre and Bell Baxter high school, all with the intention of raising the profile and uses of science in the community.

Skills for success

Being part of the academic establishment as I am, it may seem contradictory to you to learn that my career to date has relied on many skills that cannot be learned in a classroom or library. I am thinking specifically of teamwork, getting along with others and resilience. I have never viewed my education in the strictest sense as being confined to formal establishments such as school, college or university. Your education – more accurately your learning – can occur in any situation, formal or informal. When choosing three skills that have been central to my success you will see they have an application to any career and not just that of a scientist. They are the core skills of *original thinking, investigatory skills,* and *versatility.*

Original thinking

In a field of prescribed methodologies and practices, it may surprise you to learn that original thinking is a core skill of any successful scientist. It is the scientist's role to stretch the debate and challenge accepted practice; if this approach is not pursued science will never break new ground and new discoveries will be lost as a result of the same approaches producing the same results. A good illustration of this can be seen in context of laboratory experiments. When testing a question or a theory, a good scientist should experiment with his or her approach and be prepared to introduce new techniques and procedures in an effort to produce a new set of results. In this process a good scientist should always remain open minded, for what they expected to find at the outset may be totally different from the end result.

By definition, an original thinker must be independent and free of influences on their work that are not based on test data. An example of this is a challenge I made following publication of a scientific paper. The author was an established and respected scientist with an international profile. I knew their work was of a high standard and their conclusions subject to great academic rigour. From my own experience, however, I was of the opinion that the findings might be flawed. As a scientist committed to the advancement of my field, I felt I had a moral duty to challenge the findings if I believed there to be a mistake in the scientific enquiry. I could not be influenced by the author's reputation and shrink from making my challenge. I checked my argument thoroughly, for I knew it would come under great scrutiny. When it was made public, my challenge caused great debate and was ultimately well received. As a result I provided a new perspective on an established area of work, opening up the possibility of new discoveries being made through future research.

The ability to think independently is a major asset for any individual. In both our personal and professional lives we have all felt the pressure of being swept along by the tide and agreeing with others even when we know something not to be true. It takes confidence to be the only person in the room to support a particular point of view. Such people are vital, however, in helping to shine light on new areas as it often acts as a precursor to new discoveries.

Investigatory skills

I like to think of a good scientist as being like a good detective. When you start out on an enquiry you should never twist evidence to fit your own pre-determined agenda but should remain open to drawing fact-based conclusions from wherever the evidence takes you. In the context of science we have discussed how the concept of original thinking is crucial in designing experiments to explore specific theories and questions. If the experiments are designed poorly they will produce contaminated results, the publication of which would cause reputational damage for both the individual concerned and institution they represent.

The scientific community faces the same economic pressures that wider society does. Much scientific research is funded by grants, which are sums of money available from public and private sector organisations. To be awarded a grant, academic institutions must make a case for their proposed project and outline the prospective benefits to be achieved. With funding in short supply, this is a competitive process. You can therefore appreciate how financial assistance is more likely to be awarded to institutions producing consistently credible results and respected by the wider scientific community, than to those producing unreliable findings on the back of poor scientific practice. Put simply, awarding bodies want the best return for their money, and to achieve this they will only invest in institutions that demonstrate the most professional approach to their work.

To meet professional standards, scientists must be meticulous in their approach. Their work, when published, will be subject to widespread scrutiny and will either enhance or detract from the reputation of the institution they represent. Whilst good scientists will push the boundaries to incorporate new techniques and procedures in their experiments, their approach must always be underpinned by accepted scientific methodologies and practices. A good scientist does not cut corners, always interprets data fairly and draws conclusions from the facts presented.

A great way to ensure that an investigator is acting in the correct way is to have the work checked by others before publication. This is called 'peer review'. It is common practice amongst scientists to ask colleagues and team members to check and double-check the approach they have taken to ensure that the scientific process is based on sound principles. We teach undergraduates how to design their own experiments founded on the common principles of research. When assessing any colleagues' work it is against these principles that their work will be assessed, for the most basic design error at the outset can have a massive impact on the resulting data.

A good investigator will be open to challenges made by others and will welcome critiques of their work. This is a healthy and valuable approach, for when your reputation and that of the organisation you represent is at risk it is far better for errors and omissions to be identified in the safe environment of your colleagues rather than scrutinised by people you do not know. In your own career have the courage to seek out more experienced colleagues whom you respect and ask them to review your work. In a safe and honest environment this can really benefit your development, helping you to identify areas of improvement you may not have previously acknowledged.

When working in larger teams, you will come across people who view a challenge on their work as a personal attack; for some, their personal egos are closely identified with their professional reputation. Be sensitive in ensuring that your challenges, and those made against you, are made in the context of advancing your profession and your professional development. This can be best be achieved by making sure that your arguments are based on evidence that is presented in a clear manner. Never make a challenge personal. Your own integrity is crucial in this process. Always ensure that your conduct is consistent with the ethics and rules of the profession in which you find yourself. If you are seen to act with fairness, others will be more likely to act fairly with you and, most importantly, to listen to what you have to say.

Versatility

The final skill I wish to discuss is versatility - the ability to adapt effectively to new situations. Beyond working in a laboratory (which I still sometimes do), my current role incorporates many different responsibilities. I am a team leader to the extent that I am responsible for overseeing and developing the work of undergraduates and postgraduates. I am an ambassador for my university and department in the sense that I travel the world attending conferences and meeting people from others in my field. I am also a business manager, as I am responsible for writing business cases to secure grants and for managing the budget of my department effectively so that we can achieve our scientific objectives and project deliverables.

In a career where I have developed such a diverse skill set, the primary lesson I have learned is that no one approach works. Perhaps the best example of this can be seen in managing others. I am responsible for a team of scientists, all at varying stages of their career. I am also responsible for liaising with administrative staff in the university who are integral to supporting my department on a daily basis. Every individual in this team effort is different. Every individual comes to the department with his or her own set of attributes and areas for development. Nevertheless it is my responsibility to ensure that this diverse group remains motivated and works towards our common objectives. To achieve this, I must first listen to what my colleagues are saying to me. What are their concerns? What are their goals? Only then can I make a judgment about how best to communicate and deal with each person. Some will respond best to gentle nudging, whilst others may require a more blunt approach. The point is that there is no one style of management that will work for everyone, beyond always listening to your colleagues and treating everyone fairly.

Being able to adapt to differing situations has been greatly aided by my volunteering experience, and later by the opportunity to live and travel abroad. From an early age I gained experience in dealing with different people and the confidence of knowing that I could be presented with new situations and still work with others to achieve a common goal. An important aspect of this process was increasing my own resilience to setback. When faced with the unknown – whether it be working in a new place or presented with a new challenge such as managing a budget for the first time – you will most likely make mistakes or feel daunted. To minimise these feelings find people who have faced similar challenges and ask them for help. By learning from the experience of others you will often find the challenges you face are not as difficult as you first imagined.

Managing future trends

Big data

As is the case in so many other fields, the growth of technology is having a massive impact on the research of molecular biology. Perhaps the best known example of this is the genome project. The project's objective is to identify all the chemical base pairs that make up human DNA or, more simply, to map the building blocks of what makes up a human being. As you can imagine, such an undertaking requires enormous amounts of data. Whilst computers can help process this data, it remains the responsibility of scientists to collate and interpret it.

The processing power of computers should now be viewed as an integral part of any experiment. Applying the same standards as those used to assess existing scientific methods, if a computer program is configured incorrectly the data produced will equally be flawed. To be alive to this risk, scientists will increasingly need to understand the technology they are using to the same depth they do their own field of research. Having to develop this new area of expertise would clearly put an additional burden on them. To meet this challenge it is evident that educational institutions and research facilities alike will have to introduce technical awareness as a fundamental dimension on which scientists are assessed on their way to attaining a qualification.

Collaboration

The processing power of technology is helping scientists to understand the physical world better than ever before. Synergies and commonalities are being identified in all areas of science. A by-product of this emerging trend is the drawing of scientific disciplines closer together, for the expanse of data being produced dictates that any meaningful interpretation will require a multi-disciplinary approach that includes biologists, chemists, mathematicians and physicists to name but a few.

The move towards collaborative working should be seen as a positive development. By encouraging multi-disciplinary collaboration the field of microbiology has been strengthened by learning from the practices of other professionals. With greater exposure to how our colleagues approach their work, we have adopted some of their best practice and thereby enhanced our own procedures.

It also brings its own unique challenges. For example, the greater level of information-sharing between scientific fields raises challenges in terms of alignment. Both the language and scientific methodology used tends to be slightly different – a factor that has to be acknowledged when interpreting results. To be sure of a consistent approach scientists will require good leadership and team working skills, making sure that all members of the project are made to feel valued and are pulling in the same direction.

The human genome project is a great example of what can be achieved when a number of scientific disciplines harness technology to work towards a common goal. Aspiring scientists now have a responsibility to consider how their work may also be enhanced by input from other scientific disciplines.

Conclusion

When seeking employment or a place in higher education you must be honest and ask yourself what you can bring to that position. Are you a great communicator? A team player? Or a natural leader? It is important to remember that no-one is born with these skills but instead we develop them over time.

In my current role you can see that I use a variety of skills, many of which have an application beyond my core laboratory work. The development of these skills owes a lot to my broad interpretation of the concept of education. Whilst academic learning is crucial in providing a sound platform for presenting and interpreting information you will learn equally important skills outside the classroom, not least how to work well with others and adapt quickly to new environments. My voluntary work during secondary school proved to be a great experience in this regard.

Whether you are embarking on your first career, or changing to another, it is important that you do something you enjoy. This will be a combination of exercising the skills you enjoy using in a field in which you have a genuine interest. Few of us know what we want to do until we have tried a few different jobs, so do not be afraid of getting out there and becoming involved in new ventures. Again, my experiences of volunteering and the Duke of Edinburgh Scheme were invaluable in sharpening my career focus.

As my field evolves it is evident that by enabling scientific analysis to be conducted on a scale hitherto unknown, technology will bring about a great many new discoveries. This will have the attendant effect of bringing scientific disciplines closer together, as our understanding of what can be investigated grows and crosses disciplinary boundaries. As this process matures, the scientist of tomorrow has an ethical responsibility to ensure that the use of technology is understood and controlled in the same way other experimental techniques are, and are not deployed simply as a means to an end.

Chapter 5
The Tourism Director

Leslie Vella has made a significant contribution to international tourism during a career that has spanned decades and every continent of the globe.

He recently stepped down as chairman of the European Travel Commission (ETC) Market Intelligence Group, but remains a director at the Malta Tourism Authority where he also spent almost four years as chief executive officer.

His story is one of lifelong learning from around the globe.

I have to confess that I never really contemplated a job, let alone a career, in tourism. I grew up in a world of social, political and technological upheaval. I have early memories of the first satellites trekking across the night sky, manned lunar landings and the introduction of colour television. I grew up in a Mediterranean that was mostly ruled by military regimes and lived through major changes in my country's government and economy. Change has been a determining factor in my life.

On completion of my post-secondary school studies, I opted to read for a full-time BA (Hons) degree in business management at the University of Malta. At the time, Malta's university ran a system called the student-worker scheme, where students were sponsored by an employer and offered on-the-job training integrated with academic tuition. At the end of the course, graduates were offered full-time employment by the sponsoring employer. In my case I was invited for an interview at Malta's Tourism Authority, during which the challenges and attractions of a tourism career were discussed. I was subsequently sponsored by the organisation in 1983, and continue to work for it today a full thirty-one years later!

Getting work as a student is so important. It not only helps your studies but also forms your first outlook on the working world, building skills, experiences, confidence and connections. What is most important are the connections you make. If made well, the connections you establish during your early career will be returned to time and time again. Making a really good impression in early jobs can set you up brilliantly for future success. So never think a work experience placement or Saturday job is just that. It might be the start of something brilliant.

My career development in tourism

When I joined the Malta Tourism Authority I began as a trainee in the Marketing and Research Division. My work mostly dealt with collating and interpreting tourism statistics. At that time statistics were kept for records only, but today we use facts and figures about tourism far more to plan. The numbers of people travelling, how much they spend and where they go are vital pieces of information for a successful tourism industry.

Five years after my first job I was given a three-year posting as deputy director of the Malta Tourist Office in London, England. This posting had a profound effect on my personal and professional development. The impact of changing my base from one of Europe's smallest countries to one of the world's greatest cities was immense. London taught me all about independence, long hours, self-sufficiency, assertiveness and the solitude of a big place. My UK posting also improved the level of my written and spoken English, sharpened my communication skills and prepared me for the new responsibilities I was to assume upon my return to Malta.

When I returned I was given the freedom to design and build the Tourism Authority's Research Unit. I built a multi-disciplinary team with experts in market research, statistics, economics, product planning and human resources. Two of the team's greatest achievements were carrying out Malta's first ever Tourism Economic Impact Study and Tourism Carrying Capacity Assessment. The third was the launch of the Tour Operator Support Scheme, aimed at stabilising and re-growing the declining British tour operator market to Malta.

This personal success led to my career path taking an interesting and unexpected turn, when in 1999 I was appointed director of corporate services of the Tourism Authority. The role, which was mainly administrative in nature, broadened my horizons and introduced me to the world of budgeting, financial control, human resource planning, collective bargaining with trade unions, disciplinary procedure, procurement and resource allocation.

It sounds like a bureaucratic, paperwork nightmare, but I left with a superb understanding of all the things that are needed to make a large organisation work effectively. It was at this time that I also assumed chairmanship of the European Travel Commission's Market Intelligence Group. Members of this cross-European group were traditionally used to hiding information from each other. Through team working, negotiation and communication I convinced them to become a group that recognised the benefits of collaborating.

Success has the tendency to snowball. At the tender age of thirty-six years I was offered the post of chief executive officer (CEO) of the Malta Tourism Authority. I ended up in charge of an organisation of one hundred and fifty people, with offices in ten countries and an annual budget of around £20m. At that time it was the national tourism body of a destination that was attracting 1.2 million tourists annually, in an industry sustaining two hundred hotels, 45,000 licensed beds and 20,000 staff, with a full economic impact of around twenty-four per cent of Malta's gross domestic product (GDP).

I enjoyed four successful years as CEO, but decided to stand down following a major reorganisation exercise that redefined the organisation's top management structure. At that stage many assumed that it would be the end of my career at the Tourism Authority, but here I am ten years later and still with a tale to tell.

Re-inventing myself in the same organisation, in the potentially apocalyptic aftermath of my time as CEO, forced me to shift direction. I became more strategic in my outlook, drawing on the wide experience I had accumulated in my various posts. By so doing, I managed to convert what was initially an unsustainable situation into a very unique and useful one because I could contribute to the thinking and planning process in a way that no-one else could emulate.

At this point in time I continue to be valued for my strategic perspective, my research background, my verbal and written communications skills, and my ability to see supply and demand as opposite sides of the same coin. I continue to enjoy my role and feel that my contribution is not only useful but also needed.

Core skills

Five key skills have been vital to my achieving the post of CEO and continuing to enjoy success as a marketing director in the international tourism arena. The first is very much the ability to become an *international worker* and have a global perspective. The others include being part of and fostering a strong *team spirit* and engaging in *lifelong learning*. Closely linked to being a lifelong learner is the need to have a *broad spectrum of knowledge*. The final skill is one that any manager or leader of a large organisation needs, and that is the ability to be a *system-wide thinker*. Being a good team player and a good learner are easy to cultivate, but becoming a system-wide thinker and an international worker might need more planning.

Working in the international arena
This is something that any person keen on succeeding in his/her career should consider. The international arena widens perspectives, enriches experiences, exposes you not only to differences but also to similarities, and helps to enhance your network with a healthy influx of foreign contacts. Working in the international arena also forces you to shed the cloak of

insularity and parochialism. The world is a place filled with exciting and diverse people, there for anyone who wants to go out and grab it.

Living and working in a small place like Malta poses its fair share of challenges. It also has its benefits and advantages, for maybe it forced me to become international in my outlook. If you feel that there are limited opportunities for you in your local area then broaden your horizons, take a look over the parapet and get out into the big and exciting world that awaits you.

Through my work I have had the privilege of visiting around fifty different countries. I have to confess that apart from the sightseeing, my memories of most trips tend to focus more on the contacts I made, the presentations I followed and the people I met. My experience of participating in international meetings and fora has overall been positive and rewarding, becoming more so as my experience and confidence grew and my unwillingness to come out of my protective shell gradually dissipated. Thus my role has evolved naturally over time from the very reactive, background one of my early days to a more proactive, central one in the events I participate in now.

In the right environment there are no such things as language barriers, country sizes or economic might. What I have always experienced is an innate curiosity in what was being said, a constant sense of support and encouragement from my peers and the creation of long-lasting friendships and contacts that not only enrich one's life but also provide a big helping hand in one's career progression.

A rapidly changing world: the constant need to learn and unlearn
Owing to my analytical background, I have always formulated my thoughts on the basis of empirical data and facts. Armed with the unassailable comfort of data I can strongly defend my position and argue in favour of my point of view against divergent opinions.

I also possess an intense dislike of middle-of-the-road compromises. Experience has shown me time and again that compromises are nothing but stop-gap agreements that merely delay the inevitable if not actually serving to compound the problem. I would rather argue my position and enjoy an open debate until the discussion is exhausted and a decision is taken based on the strongest argument. Experience has also shown me that systems that function on the basis of weak compromises suffer in the long term. Such behaviour only serves to further weaken the usefulness of what I call 'patched' solutions, which in my view are ultimately no solutions at all.

To summarise, I prefer an approach where I first formulate an opinion on the basis of a thorough analysis of the situation, backed up by good data; this allows me to be confident of my position and receptive to it being tested against divergent viewpoints. I would always rather concede defeat in the face of a stronger argument than seek half-baked solutions.

Being able to form opinions that are backed up by data rather than based on whims or gut feelings, necessitates a capacity to learn. In my case, learning is a process that never ceases. I have known people who decided to stop learning at a certain point in their lives on the arrogant assumption that there is nothing left for them to learn, i.e. they know everything there is to know. I consider this a sad predicament and the starting phase of mental *rigor mortis*. Learning is a lifelong process that requires the right attitude, is constantly fuelled by curiosity and reflects a wish to absorb more of what is going on around you.

Learning is also an integral part of the process of enriching and consolidating our fundamental beliefs - as long as it is never approached in a dogmatic manner; our constantly changing world does not respond well to rigid dogmatism, tending to ride roughshod over those unwilling to be flexible. It adds to and strengthens our body of knowledge, thereby allowing deeper consideration of a subject. Furthermore, the expansion of knowledge both horizontally and vertically enables all-important inter-linkages to be established. My career in tourism has taught me the need to interlink seemingly mutually exclusive concepts. Interlinking helps me to see the wider picture, which typically exceeds the sum of its parts. Thus learning is fundamental to acquiring the capacity to interlink.

While unashamedly extolling the virtues of learning as a constant and ongoing process, I also believe in the process I call 'unlearning'. The term is inspired by computer-age terminology such as 'undo' and 'unlike', and in my case consists of the capacity constantly to review one's body of knowledge and jettison overboard anything that might be considered obsolete or superfluous to requirement. Learning and unlearning go hand in hand: that which is currently more relevant to what is taking place needs to overwrite, rather than be stored next to, that which is no longer useful.

Unlearning can be seen as a fundamental part of one's constant adaptation to change, shedding what is no longer relevant and replacing it with that which is. It is part of the evolution of thought and, being based on the principle of evolution, allows change to be incorporated in a way that still bears a relationship, albeit distant, with one's past beliefs and attitudes.

Fostering a team spirit

Over the years I have acquired a lot of international experience of working with different groups of people. The bulk of this experience has come from seventeen years chairing the European Travel Commission's Market Intelligence Group. The Group's core members comprise the research directors of thirty-three European national tourism administrations, but it also encompasses a network of other researchers from the World Tourism Organisation, European Cities Marketing and the European Tour Operators Association. It is a challenging role that requires a tough balancing act to manage the formalities of getting a number of international associations to work together, the problems posed by language barriers in a forum that depends on English as the language of communication, and the need to generate practical and timely outputs for internal and global stakeholders.

In presiding over the Group I have, over the years, developed an approach that uses informality to get the best from its members while maintaining a business-like approach to decisions around work quality, budgets and deadlines. The result is an informal setting that is conducive to decision-making and generates high quality outputs. The impact of this achievement can only be fully appreciated when one considers that the group comprises members of different nationalities and different sectoral backgrounds who are traditionally used to competing rather than co-operating with each other. My overall philosophy with respect to fostering a team spirit in all the groups that I have had the privilege to lead can be condensed into the following points:

- For the good of the group and the professionalism of its output one must always seek the right balance between procedure and practicality. Procedure provides peace of mind but stifles flexibility. Practicality gives a lot of freedom but needs to be handled responsibly and with strong leadership.
- While decision-making deadlines are there to be respected in as practical a way as possible I would never stifle the opinion of any member, even if it arrives at the eleventh

hour or later. This is what keeps participation in the group dynamic and sustainable in the long term.

- When faced with tight situations, I prefer to give the heart precedence over the mind. Teams and groups generally comprise sets of highly focused, intelligent, expert, trustworthy and unbiased professionals whose aggregate brain power supersedes the cold, numeric data of a printed sheet of paper full of numbers. This is what differentiates humans from machines. Thus, for example, when an evaluation grid points to broad consensus, use it; when it provides a muddled picture you can choose to keep struggling with what will remain a muddled picture, or dump it and start talking.
- In situations where no clear decisions can be taken, seek the comfort of previous experience if the situation allows it. When in a tied situation give precedence and preference to the devil you know. Doing so sweetens the bitterness of fear of risk.
- Put forward all your arguments for and against a motion, but always with a view to seeking consensus. A change of opinion following a reasoned discussion is not a sign of weakness but a sign of superior mental processing. I have always preferred changing people's opinions to obtain agreement over decisions based on simple majorities. We should all be winners after a decision is taken.

Future skills

Having the luxury of being able to look back over a long career in some privileged roles in tourism gives me an interesting viewpoint from which to consider the future. I said earlier that I think system-wide thinking is vital to the workforce of the future, and I go on to describe what I mean by that in more detail in this final section. A further 'future skill' is the ability to gain, retain and use a wide spectrum of knowledge. In a world where people work in so many different areas, in different teams and with different people, it is important to have a wide spectrum of knowledge and know how to apply it to different places, people and situations. A final piece of advice for anyone looking to the future would be to find and use a good mentor. You cannot do it all yourself and there are plenty of people out there well equipped to help you on your journey.

The importance of a wide spectrum of knowledge

As my career has developed I have reaped numerous benefits from the fact that I possess a wide spectrum of knowledge. I believe that knowledge is useful for any career, but it is definitely an important pre-requisite for something as complex and multi-disciplinary as tourism.

Since my childhood I have had a strong interest in astronomy. This lifelong hobby has helped me to appreciate the fact that understanding astronomy necessitates a broad understanding and interlinking of a range of subjects. The same applies to tourism. In fact, I attribute my successful career in tourism precisely to the capacity to follow and understand a wide range of subjects that I acquired during my amateur astronomy days.

Understanding tourism primarily requires one to appreciate that human activity is not always logical but depends heavily on emotions and other irrational behaviours. This requires some familiarity with diverse disciplines such as anthropology, sociology, human geography and psychology. As a business activity, tourism also calls for a solid grounding in macro- and micro-economics, while a foundation in commerce and finance helps one to get to grips with the mechanisms governing companies in these industries. The demand side of the industry also necessitates a degree of competence in marketing, and with e-commerce replacing traditional business models in tourism faster in the tourism industry than in any other sector, a knowledge of information technology is becoming more and more important.

Nor does it end there. Being a good tourism manager requires a broad understanding of the supply side of the industry: from building design and planning requirements to issues of quality and standards. Tourism supply also includes accommodation, catering establishments, entertainment and meeting facilities, visitor attractions and the commercialisation of various different products and services for consumption by tourists. Some familiarity with relevant pieces of legislation is also useful to further complete the picture.

Looking to the destination itself, familiarity with its natural and man-made environments can be helpful in understanding what constitutes its competitive advantages, as can a solid grounding in the history and culture, potential, carrying capacity and constraints of a destination. Recognising that one is competing against an almost infinite variety of alternative destinations necessitates that one also understands the competition's offer.

The above list shows the diverse and interesting range of subjects that a serious and professional tourism manager needs to grasp in order to gain a broader understanding of something as seemingly unsophisticated as tourism. Obviously the very breadth of the list implies that one cannot gain in-depth, expert knowledge of every discipline: that is where the specialists come in. Nevertheless, from the very outset the ability to understand, connect and inter-link all the above subjects, and many others too minor to include here, is in my opinion a skill that no tourism manager can afford not to possess.

System-wide thinking

As a child I was enchanted by astronomy, an interest that was to have great bearing on my attitude towards life and my eventual career for two major reasons. First of all, understanding astronomy necessitated a broad understanding and interlinking of a spectrum of subjects, from the traditional sciences, through geography and geology and extending into the realms of cosmology and philosophical thought. The second reason lies in the fact that astronomy was and continues to be a rapidly evolving subject, thanks to the constant flow of new discoveries and interpretations that see established theories rise and fall. A broad spectrum of knowledge, the ability to make inter-linkages and to adapt to constant change: all are attributes that I have found consistently useful in the thirty-one years of my tourism career.

People working in organisations need to appreciate that single decisions or actions in one place have an impact on other people and other things in that organisation. This can be hard to appreciate, until you find yourself working with large and complex organisations. To illustrate this a simple picture to draw in your head is the game of Jenga, where moving one block in the pile can have an impact somewhere else in the tower even though you did not mean for it to happen.

The modern workplace needs people who can see the big picture and risk-assess decisions before they take them. Astronomy helped me to understand this, while for others it was playing football manager games on the computer. Here too, one action can have a major impact: buying one player can lead to another leaving, while making a substitution at the right time can change the whole game. The best way to develop system-wide thinking is to experience it, whether it be through strategy or sports manager games or through interest in real life subjects like astronomy or the natural world around us.

Mentors

Across my thirty-one year career I have been privileged to receive mentoring and tutoring from some very experienced people, whose influence on the way I think and act today is something I recognise and appreciate.

In retrospect, what these great people were doing was imparting their accumulated body of knowledge to me and my peers, thus ensuring that what they themselves had learned - either through personal experience or from what others had passed on to them - would be passed on to the next generation. When one has the good fortune to work in the same organisation for thirty-plus years, one encounters the surreal situation of working with fellow employees who had not been born when you first started working there! This makes you appreciate the length of your relationship with your job and your responsibility in passing the baton of acquired knowledge to the next generation.

I am a strong believer in mentoring, having benefited from powerful and effective mentoring myself in the initial stages of my career development. Mentoring is different from indoctrination in that it teaches one how to think rather than what to think. I like to think that my current thoughts are my own, but I also acknowledge the people who taught me to come up with them.

Conclusion

Ultimately, I owe my success to the knowledge and opportunities that others have given me. I feel obliged to continue this cycle with the next generation of work colleagues, whom I see not as threats to be feared but as resources that should be nurtured and fed to become stronger until the time comes for them to take over.

Two quotes have stuck with me all my life. The first is Galileo Galilei's, *'Eppur si muove (nevertheless it moves)'*, a masterpiece of resilience and strength of character in the face of adversity. The second is Sir Isaac Newton's, *'If I have seen further it is by standing on the shoulders of giants.'*

Chapter 6
The Doctor

Angela Davidson is a paediatric doctor. She completed two degree courses to achieve her dream.

Amongst her other achievements she has worked overseas in Peru providing healthcare to poverty-stricken communities. As well as achieving success in the medical world, Angela now also works as a university clinical tutor, helping to inform and inspire the next generation of medics.

Her story is one of resilience and commitment, not just to achieving her dream but also to helping others to overcome life's challenges.

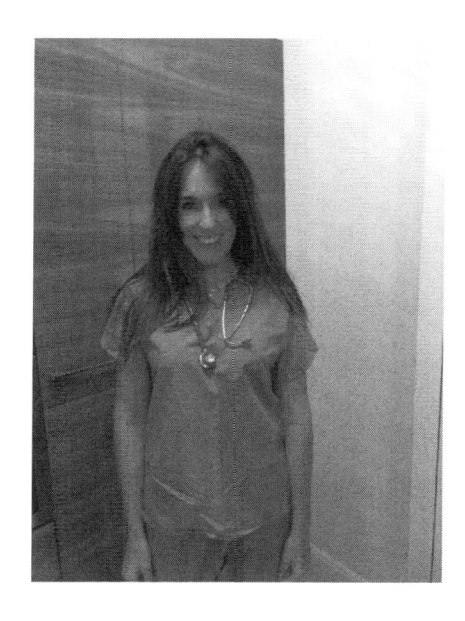

It is 3.17am and I can hear the familiar noise of my pager relentlessly screaming in the pocket of my scrubs. There are numerous other monitors sounding off around me. The environment is busy and noisy. I cannot quite reach the pager to silence it as I have my hands in the incubator of a three-month-old premature baby weighing little more than 1lb, trying to take blood. I need to get to the phone to see what the next emergency is. '*Hi, it's Angela the Neonatal Registrar...*' Every now and then the words echo in my mind as if unreal. This is not really me, is it? How on earth did I get here?!

My name is Angela Davidson and I am a doctor. I specialise in paediatrics, which means helping babies and children get better. I currently work in a neonatal intensive care unit looking after sick and premature babies. I have wanted to be a doctor for as long as I can remember, but while at school I never considered this career a possibility for a number of reasons. I wish to use this article to chart my journey to becoming a doctor. Specifically I hope to highlight the reality of being a doctor and the skills that are vital to my profession. I will then finish the discussion by identifying the skills that will be in most demand in the medical profession of tomorrow.

My path to becoming a doctor

My journey has been somewhat protracted, which I think helps me to be a better clinician. I have spent eight years at university studying for two degrees, but it has certainly been worth it. I love my job and enjoy the endless challenges medicine throws at me. Alongside hospital work I am employed as a university clinical tutor, helping to educate the next generation of doctors. I have been actively involved in research and have just finished editing the neonatal chapter of a medical text book. In 2012 I spent ten days in remote regions of north Peru with an American charity providing healthcare and medicines to poverty-stricken communities. It is certainly fair to say that my job has the potential to take me all over the world and no two days are the same.

There are lots of different types of doctor and you choose what specialty within medicine appeals to you after medical school. Some doctors enjoy the variety that comes with being a general practitioner (GP) or family doctor working in the community, whereas others enjoy hospital-based medicine and so decide to become a surgeon or a medical physician. There are dozens of specialties to choose from, certain ones being more competitive than others. Some doctors have more limited patient access and prefer instead to be involved in teaching, research or public health. It is a very varied career and most people entering the profession find an area they are interested in and are passionate about.

The public's perception of the medical profession is varied. Doctors were once held in high regard: trusted and respected. Today, a lot of frustration with access to services, waiting lists and potentially unhelpful tabloid headlines suggesting that doctors are underworked and overpaid has eroded public faith in the medical profession. I certainly did not enter medicine for the money and do not believe that many of my colleagues did either. If you are looking for a 'get rich quick' career then medicine probably is not for you. My friends working in investment banking in the City make infinitely more than I do. Whilst medicine is reasonably well paid, to be a really good doctor you must be willing to pledge a lifetime commitment to caring for your patients. The entry requirements are academically tough, the hours are long, the job is busy and often you do not get appreciation or recognition for your work. It can also be emotionally heart-breaking. You are exposed to people at their most vulnerable and often during the worst times of their lives. Although you need to retain some emotional distance for your own sake, I challenge anyone not to be affected by a lot of what we deal with on a daily basis and I can certainly recall a few instances of arriving home in a haze of tears after witnessing particularly distressing situations.

Medicine does take over your life. By virtue of the number of hours you spend around fellow medics, many of your friends will be doctors. Your partner may well be a doctor too! When your non-medic friends are having a night out at the weekend you may not be able to go because you are working. So medicine is not just a career choice, it is a lifestyle choice. That is not to say that you cannot have interests outside medicine – quite the opposite. Because of the career's demands, doctors usually enjoy busy social lives and a range of hobbies to counteract the pressures of work. Certain medical specialties are more family-friendly than others, so it is certainly the case that most people can find a career path to fit with other life goals such as starting a family and wanting to work part time. Despite medicine's demands there is not a single other job I would rather have. Being a doctor is challenging, interesting, rewarding and a privilege.

So what was it about medicine that initially appealed to me? My first memory of considering the career was whilst sitting in my local GP practice, waiting to visit my family doctor. I think I was around ten years old at the time. The doctor was a friendly man who was clever and knew how to make me feel better which I found very impressive! Since then I thought it must be amazing to be able to be a doctor, but I never seriously considered it as a career option for me. My mum died suddenly when I was eleven years old and during my teenage years I lacked any clear focus. As I progressed through secondary school and exams I was good academically but not outstanding. I did not have much of an interest in science so I scraped a couple of A's and B's in arts subjects and went off to university to study psychology. It was very interesting but I could not help but envy my friends studying for their medical degrees. They would work very hard but also had a great camaraderie, and I decided medicine was the career I wanted to follow.

After graduating with my honours degree I knew medicine was a possibility for postgraduates but felt I needed a break from studying, at least for a while. I began working as a nursing assistant in a psychiatric unit to get a feel for whether medicine or psychology was the right career path for me. Very quickly I knew I really wanted to be a doctor. I found I was very good at interacting with patients and I enjoyed the hospital environment. I also discovered that I really wanted to know more about the pathology of illnesses and had a real interest in their acute medical management. That fascinated me much more than other aspects of their care such as rehabilitation or counselling, which are just as important but not something that appealed to me. I set about gaining work experience at a GP practice and local teaching hospital then applied once again to university, this time to study medicine. I was delighted to be accepted on a four-year graduate course.

Often students apply to study medicine because their parents are doctors or because they achieved straight A's at school. There is nothing wrong with that as long as it is not your only reason for choosing medicine and you have a real desire to become a doctor. If you are not sure whether it is the right choice, get some work experience in a hospital environment. One of the entrance requirements for medical school is displaying a commitment to the profession, and a good understanding of what is involved in the day to day job is essential. I love being around people and pride myself in understanding others and having genuine empathy. When something is wrong I immediately want to find a solution and make somebody feel better. Sometimes it is not possible to fix something, but if you are the type of person who genuinely cares and would naturally put an arm round another person because they are hurting you have the potential to be a good doctor.

The doctor's skill set

Passion and compassion

There are a number of skills you need in order to pursue medicine, but I believe one of the most important traits is passion. Medicine is academically tough but requires enthusiasm and a willingness to work hard more than necessarily being naturally clever. Essential academic requirements for school-leavers are high and typically require A grades in a range of subjects including the sciences. You also need to have an appreciation of core maths in order to calculate drugs, doses and concentrations. Graduates can apply with an Honours degree at 2.1 or above with little or no science background. Just be prepared to dedicate your life to studying – especially during the first year. There is a lot to learn and many of the concepts require a detailed level of understanding, but dedication and a keen interest in what you are studying will get most people through the degree. It is only once you graduate from medical school that the real education on how to be a doctor begins. Having passion for medicine means that despite the hard work and tough demands you continue to give 100 per cent whilst at the same time enjoying the challenge.

As previously stated, it is vital to be able to show compassion and have good communication skills. This can be taught and further developed at medical school but it is important to be a people person from the outset. That certainly does not mean that you have to be loud and outgoing. Medicine attracts all types of personalities, and as long as you have time for people and a caring nature you will have a good foundation. Most medical specialties require a lot of people contact. Having a good 'bedside manner' is vital in building trust with patients. Encounters vary from congratulating a couple on the birth of their healthy baby, to trying to tease out the real fears and anxieties of a patient who really wants to disclose feelings of depression but initially claims to be seeking treatment for a sore arm. Unfortunately we also have to break bad news such as a diagnosis of cancer or the death of a loved one.

Resilience

Even when life is at its toughest for your patients you can still make a positive impact if bad news is delivered in the right way. Sometimes as a doctor you might have numerous consultations within a short space of time. Some may be positive and others very difficult, but it is necessary to maintain a professional composure regardless of what you are dealing with or despite the previous discussion you have just had. A friend who is not a doctor told me that he thought resilience was an important characteristic of being a doctor, and I think that is a very astute observation even if we do not feel it is the case at times. Medicine does expose you to a range of very difficult situations and having a strong support network or other means of stress management is vitally important. This can often be developed between doctors and is one reason why there tends to be such camaraderie between medics.

Problem-solving

One of my early medical tutors once claimed that medicine is more of an art than a science. I thought this was a strange comment as I naively believed medicine was an exact discipline with right and wrong answers. Since then I have reflected on how true his statement is. Rarely is medicine black and white. Patients often do not present with typical textbook histories to suggest a diagnosis, and clinicians can disagree over the best way to proceed. To be a doctor is to be a problem solver and have an inquisitive mind. Often we are required to 'think outside the box' in order to diagnose and treat a patient. Even if someone presents with what initially appears to be a straightforward complaint, there are often multiple factors to take into account. Consider for example a small child who presents with bruises. They might be distressed and crying but, depending on their age, might be too young to say what is wrong. There are multiple causes of bruises on a small child, ranging from normal accidental bruising to leukaemia and child abuse. The first is by far the most common diagnosis, but the second two are serious and essential not to miss. Having an open mind, always considering alternatives and constantly asking, 'Have I got this right?' are crucial. This type of interrogating mind is fundamental to the art of medicine.

Teamwork

To be any kind of doctor you have to interact well in a team. No medic is able to work independently and most doctors rely on several members within a multi-disciplinary team to comprehensively treat a patient. We work closely with numerous other health professionals and anyone involved in a patient's life can potentially be involved in their healthcare. As a doctor it is vital to appreciate and assimilate the contribution of all the individuals involved.

An elderly person who has a fall at home and breaks their hip bone offers a good example. The orthopaedic surgeon is responsible for mending the broken bone, but that is merely the start of the patient's recovery. Radiographers take the initial x-rays that allow doctors to make the diagnosis. Laboratory technicians process blood samples to ensure that a patient is fit for surgery. Porters ensure the safe transport of the patient to the operating theatre for their surgery and back to the ward. Pharmacists ensure that medications are prescribed correctly and that there are no adverse interactions with new medication. Nurses care for the patient on the ward, attending to their day-to-day needs including washing, feeding and ensuring that they take their medications. Physiotherapists are responsible for helping the patient to become more mobile by creating sets of exercises to gradually build up strength. The hospital chaplains are important for the patient's religious and spiritual needs. Dieticians may become involved if there are nutritional concerns, which are not uncommon in older and frail patients. Occupational therapists may make home visits to decide if any environmental adaptations might expedite discharge from hospital, and social workers may co-ordinate care packages to meet the patient's needs following discharge.

The list of people in the hospital team is endless. Wards are busy places and it is essential to use and respect the expertise of all the clinical teams in order to provide the best care for patients. Teamwork and communication are therefore paramount.

Commitment to excellence

I and many of my fellow medics have perfectionist personalities and pay great attention to detail which I certainly think helps to become a good doctor. Most doctors are not satisfied with doing an 'ok' job for their patients and are prepared to go above and beyond to help someone. My hours are certainly not nine-to-five and often I leave work hours late because I want to make sure I have done the best job for my patients. There are also a lot of demands placed on doctors beyond the clinical mandate. Often you are expected at short notice to organise teaching, become involved in research, give impromptu presentations or cover another doctor's workload for whatever reason.

Despite the extra demands and stress, most doctors will continue to give 100 per cent and ensure that their work, regardless of the role they are fulfilling, is done to the best of their ability. Attention to detail goes hand in hand with this approach, as it ensures that any task is undertaken comprehensively. Consider a baby born very prematurely. This kind of case involves a lot of work for the medical team. There is often a considerable number of practical procedures to be undertaken to stabilise the baby. They often need to be intubated (have a breathing tube inserted) and placed on a ventilator, require intravenous lines to be placed, have x-rays and scans performed, have drugs and antibiotics written up and their notes completed. It is also essential to keep an open mind about their condition. Observations such as their heart rate and oxygen level need to be monitored, and the many complications of prematurity constantly considered and investigated where appropriate. It is also vital to keep the baby's parents constantly updated. All these tasks are of equal importance and completing them often requires multi-tasking. To ensure that everything is done well and to the high standard expected of a doctor, we must have the type of personality that demands the best of ourselves at all times.

Medicine is certainly a challenge in many regards, but I believe it is absolutely worth it. I think going in as a graduate with a bit more life experience helped me, but I also believe that most of my younger colleagues have the maturity to equip them for the profession. If I could rewind the clock I would certainly have focused more at school and believed in myself from a younger age. Anything is possible if you have the drive. I would have found medical school easier with a better knowledge base of science, but nothing is impossible with hard work and determination.

Future skills

Attention to detail
Attention to detail is a key skill that will become ever more important in the medical profession. I previously alluded to it when discussing the importance of a commitment to excellence, but I think the significance of thorough and meticulous practice will only increase in the future. It is not sufficient to have a vague grasp of the current situation of your patients, particularly when they are in hospital. Very small changes in blood results or fluctuations in observations may be a sign of something clinically significant and must be identified by the doctor. You are required to have a detailed knowledge of all your patients' care and constantly be attending to various aspects of their treatment.

As knowledge advances, more and more doctors are becoming increasingly sub-specialised because there is simply too much detail to know for them to remain generalised. This has its advantages and disadvantages. It means that specialists can pursue their own specific interests and thus be experts in their field and help to contribute to advancements. On the flip side it is important for certain clinicians, particularly GPs, to be able to maintain a broad overview of all aspects of their patients' lives in order to ensure a holistic approach to their care. If you enjoy learning about something in great detail or take pride in ensuring that everything is as it should be in the projects you undertake, you may have the right mindset to pursue medicine.

An inquisitive mind

The future of medicine is very exciting. Advances in treatments and new research findings are published every day. I believe another key skill for doctors over the coming years and decades will be an inquisitive mind and the desire to answer some of the many questions that remain unanswered in medicine. Even well-established treatments can always be improved upon, but it requires the active pursuit of new knowledge.

It can be easy to rely on tried and tested methods and treatments, but to be a doctor who makes a great discovery is to be a doctor who will be remembered in generations to come. Patients now demand more and more of their doctors and treatments. Not everyone can make innovative breakthroughs, but if clinicians have the thirst and drive to improve practice then the profession will continue to advance.

As the specialty that has advanced the most in recent times, neonatology is probably the best illustration of this. Just thirty years ago, within my lifetime, if you were a baby born extremely prematurely your chances of survival were slight; if you did survive, your chances of having a significant neuro-developmental disability were high. We have since learned a lot about supporting extreme preterm babies and the gestational limits of viability are continually being challenged. We have discovered medicines to help babies' lungs, have improved ventilation equipment to breathe for them and are developing strategies to treat many of the complications of prematurity. We also know more about how to help full-term babies who have sustained a brain injury, such as cooling them for a short period in order to protect their brain and reduce the incidence of cerebral palsy.

We have even developed transport teams throughout the country capable of delivering intensive care in ambulances, helicopters and aeroplanes. This means that patients in more remote locations can be transferred to tertiary units in order to receive specialist and/or high-tech intensive care during transport.

Each small element of these advances required the identification of a problem, the desire to improve the current situation, an idea of how things could be made better and then rigorous trials to produce an evidence base for the new concept. There are lots of unanswered questions in every medical specialty. Cures for various diseases still need to be discovered and the science of various symptoms and illnesses is still poorly understood. What would be your interest and what discovery might you make?

Conclusion

I am excited about the future of my career. At present I am working towards becoming a consultant paediatrician and am still deciding whether I want to specialise in a particular area within paediatrics. There is a lot of autonomy in medicine in terms of taking your career down a specific route. I hope to develop my teaching role in the university over the coming academic years, but my focus will be on my clinical role. My specialty is hospital-based medicine and I appreciate that it means I will continue to work nights and weekends for the foreseeable future. I hope to contribute further to research on paediatrics, helping to improve care for babies and children in years to come through greater understanding of diseases and the development of treatments. I would also like to continue with charity work in the future, perhaps at some point down the line even volunteering with agencies such as Médecins Sans Frontières, which is an international, medical humanitarian organisation providing healthcare in some of the world's most challenging environments.

Make sure that you fully research the medical profession before deciding to become a doctor and ensure that you are doing it for the right reasons. Medicine is a wonderful career but you only get out what you put in. I have a great life outside my profession, and although most of those nearest and dearest to me are not doctors my career is certainly a significant part of my life. Colleagues tell me that I always have a smile on my face and look happy, and I believe that is because I am fortunate enough to have found my true vocation. Talk to a range of doctors about what their day-to-day job is really like and find out the aspects of the role they find toughest and most rewarding. Also, make sure you get experience of a hospital environment in order to know if it really is right for you. Once you embark on medicine be sure to give it your all. If it is as good to you as it has been to me you will find yourself in a wonderful career full of possibilities, motivation and challenges, surrounded by people who may just remember you for the rest of their lives as someone who made a positive difference.

Chapter 7
The Media Producer and Director

Keith Girdwood is a highly experienced producer/director and project manager providing digital media solutions in Scotland. Running his own business, his services range from producing video and digital content to delivering technical solutions for conferences and designing commercial, web-based applications.

In a period of economic uncertainty Keith has continued to grow his business by serving a diverse range of clients that includes the NHS, education organisations and major energy providers in the private sector. His story is all the more engaging as his business and technical skills are almost entirely self-taught.

My career has definitely not been mapped out. Instead, the choices that have brought me to where I am now have largely been based on instinct and seizing opportunities when they appeared. I would like to use this article first to explore my entry into the working world and consider how the concept of education only really begins for some once they leave school. I would then like to discuss the three skills that have been central to my success and those that will be required to succeed in my future marketplace.

My journey

Some people may think that having been privately educated as a child gave me an advantage in the early years of my development. It did: but not in the way you might think! I was placed in a peer group of individuals who came from very successful families and were well-connected to prominent people. As a result *their* careers were already largely mapped out, whether it be a position in the family business or the path to a professional career through university. As a consequence, some were apathetic about applying themselves to their studies. They had no drive because their choices had already been made for them.

I did not come from such a background. My parents made real sacrifices so that I could receive a private education. As a child, however, it is easy and even natural to become caught up in the group mentality. Like my peers, I too chose to have fun rather than attend to my academic studies. By the time I came to leave school, I realised that the academic route of going onto university and perhaps attaining a 'professional' job in an accountancy or law firm was not for me. It simply would not have made me happy. I enjoyed working with my hands and understood that something more vocational would best suit my natural skills and interests.

Looking back, I acknowledge that I did get swept up with the crowd in having too much fun at school, but I am also proud that I had the strength of character at a young age to take my life in the direction I wanted it to go. At the age of seventeen I therefore left school and took a job as a shelf-stacker at a local supermarket.

At this point you may be thinking about the reaction of my parents to this career decision. You would be correct in thinking that it created some tension! This was especially true for my father, who had come through the academic route himself. It was a difficult situation. I understood that my parents had sacrificed a lot so that I could be privately educated with the express intention of my attending university thereafter. From one perspective, however, my school experience had been valuable because it helped me identify what I did *not* want to do, which was precisely to follow the accepted route of my peers into higher education: I was learning to become my own man.

Starting at the bottom of the supermarket food chain, I stacked shelves, emptied lorries, filled freezers (a really tough job) and cut the leaves from cabbages! The work was hard and far from glamorous. I enjoyed the experience, however, and quickly appreciated how the world of work was providing me with an altogether different education. I was working with a diverse group of individuals on a range of tasks, from liaising with customers in the front store to sorting out deliveries in the back. Perhaps it was the frenetic energy of the environment or the fact that I was relying on my team working and communication skills which had never really been tested at school, but I quickly found that I had an aptitude for the work and was really enjoying the experience.

Remember I said at the start of the article that I developed my career through instinct and seizing opportunities? Well, that dynamic was about to serve me well. Through my industry and attitude I quickly moved through a number of different jobs in the supermarket. Still applying my now characteristic level of energy I was fast acquiring a reputation as someone who could 'get things done'. As a result, my boss quickly recognised my potential and put me forward for a management training programme - an unheard of opportunity for an 18-year-old.

You may ask if I felt the pressure of expectation and responsibility? The truth is, my natural instincts created a tremendous intellectual curiosity to understand how things worked. The ability to take on a number of seconded management roles was therefore liberating because I had the power to start making significant changes to how we worked as a team. So I embraced the position of manager and did not have time to think about any of the negative pressures.

At twenty-one years old I was made the youngest supermarket manager in the country and put in charge of over one hundred and fifty-five people. At twenty-two years old I was named manager of the year and put forward for a national prize. My success had been rapid. You may even say the chill of my experience working in the freezers had barely thawed! The most important point, however, was that during the same period of time (four years), while my peers from school were receiving their degree education at university I was learning about teamwork, building client relationships and getting the best out of others in an environment that had real consequences.

Having the courage to take your own path
At this juncture I would like to emphasise that I am not denigrating university or academic work. That path offers a great learning experience and is valuable in a number of fields. It simply was not the best educational environment for bringing out *my* core skills and providing *me* with the sense of achievement I was looking for. I am glad I had the strength of character to realise this at seventeen years old. Incidentally, you may also be wondering if my relationship with my parents improved as I became more successful? It did. My father in particular came to see how my decision to leave school at seventeen years of age had led to an enjoyable and successful career. I think any parent just wants their child to have the best start in life that leads to a well-paid job. If you find yourself in a similar situation where your parents wish you to take a different path, I would suggest you be honest with them about where you want to go and why. It is your life after all and you who will have to live with the consequences.

As my career in the supermarket developed I was beginning to ask questions about my future. Specifically I had the self-awareness to notice that there were very few managers with grey hair! Put simply, the frenetic pace and shift-work of supermarket life made the industry a young person's game. I also questioned where more success would take me – most likely into an office position, which was the opposite of the hands-on, vocational career path I was looking for.

A change in direction
At the same time as my supermarket career was progressing, my intellectual curiosity for understanding how things worked almost inevitably brought me into the realm of information technology (IT). In the early 1990s, the commercialisation of IT meant that it was increasingly becoming part of everyday life. These advances, typified by the move from VHS cassette to digital versatile disc (DVD) and the rise of the internet, I viewed as challenges to see how far they could be pushed. My interest was drawn primarily to the visual side of technology. I became engrossed in how to upload images more effectively. This soon branched into web development, whose commercial application for businesses advertising and selling their products I understood.

As with my career in the supermarket, my passion for IT soon brought other like-minded individuals into my orbit. It was not long before I was offered an opportunity to become involved in digital media. I jumped at the chance. Though taking a hit in wages again, my natural instincts were pulling me in a definite direction and it felt wrong to make any other choice. I particularly enjoyed the visual and creative side of my new position, and soon I was specialising in making interactive DVDs and providing services to a wide range of clients. As e-commerce grew I was conscious of the general lack of understanding amongst businesses about what could be achieved and at what cost. I quickly resolved to build a reputation on honesty and delivering practical solutions. This approach paid off and I began to form a network of business contacts who valued both my technical delivery and trustworthy advice. When I was made redundant in 2012, my reputation in the industry made it relatively easy for me to start my own business.

In truth, it was a natural progression. I now had the managerial skills and life experience honed from my early days in the supermarket right through to working in digital media to make my venture a success. So what are these three skills? More than any others I would say that *people skills*, *resilience* and *self-belief* have been central to my progression and success.

My skills for success

People skills

This is a broad term, but for me it is about being able to listen to and motivate others. From my experience of being a manager in the supermarket I quickly realised that each individual member of the team brought a different skill set to the equation. As a manager it was my responsibility to identify the strengths of each individual and put these to work, while also constructively addressing their weaknesses. For example, if I observed a colleague in the supermarket who was uncomfortable dealing with clients I would rotate them to a back office position. I would explain my reasons for doing so to the individual, ask what position they were most interested in and work towards developing their skill set in that regard. The key aspect is understanding how other people will feel about or perceive the decisions you make that affect them and still making them feel valued.

It is remarkable, looking back, how many of my managerial skills were learned at such a young age. I was fortunate in that my colleagues came from such a diverse range of backgrounds. I had students, part-time workers, and senior citizens who were looking to supplement their income, to name but a few. No one communication style worked other than being a good listener and being open to the points of view of others. Perhaps by being a manager at such a young age I was particularly sensitive to valuing the experience of others, many of whom had been doing the job much longer than I had.

From being in charge of one hundred and fifty-five people at twenty-one, to having only two people in my team a decade later in the media industry, I learned that the principles of fairness and consistency are just as important no matter how many people you lead. I class this as a *people skill*, for often the message you send out as a leader reflects back on you. Any sense of injustice, from being seen to favour others or adhering to a different set of standards, can quickly grow into resentment and stop people working for you. I believe I was able to motivate others precisely because I demonstrated the same set of values and commitment to hard work that I wished to see in them.

Resilience

It does not matter if you get it wrong. Learn from the mistake and try again. Just keep going forward. In my opinion *resilience* is the ability to keep moving forward in the face of obstacles and adversity. To advance you cannot let your mistakes define you. So often I see entrepreneurs quit after their first venture fails and return to the enterprise/job they left in the first place. What they should really do is ask why their venture failed, seek not to repeat the same mistake and try again.

Looking at my own experience I have no doubt that some viewed my path from private school to shelf-stacker as a failure. That was their perspective, not mine. From the point of view of my own career development I was making my own choices and was committed to learn from each experience. Even the most basic tasks, such as unloading lorries and filling freezers, brought me new skills that would help me compete in the wider world. I did not want to stay doing these tasks so I embraced change when the opportunity arose.

Resilience is much like the physical concept of stamina. The more you expose yourself to change and setback, your ability to handle criticism and obstacles increases; you toughen up. It therefore takes a certain amount of bravery first to put yourself in positions where you may 'fail' and second to find the drive to push through that uncertainty. In my career, intellectual curiosity to understand how things worked provided me with that drive. A good example is my career change into the media industry. My technical ability in developing websites was entirely self-taught. I simply had a burning desire to understand more, bought books on the subject and learned through trial and error. The key point is that when you have a genuine interest for a subject your enthusiasm does not let you focus or dwell on the negative. As such you are most likely to be a success in ventures in which you enjoy exercising the skills you are using and are passionate about the subject matter.

Self-belief

The final skill, that of self-belief, is related to resilience but is not the same. If you have any doubt about what you are doing you will interpret any setback as validation that you do not have what it takes. Self-belief is an antidote to these feelings of inadequacy and vital if you are to persevere and be a success.

So how do you build self-belief? Perhaps the most important aspect is preparation. For any venture in life there will be unexpected events that throw up obstacles in your way. No amount of preparation will reduce all risk to zero, but by knowing your subject matter well you should be able not only to cope effectively but to turn a problem to your advantage. I strongly believe that adversity brings out the best forms of innovation. When starting out on your own money can be tight. You are therefore forced to maximise the potential of the resources available. A good example of this was early in my media career when I was using ineffective keyboard commands for a program. Faced with the prospect of spending money for repairs, I simply used the touch screen facility and crafted an application to replace the function of the keyboard.

I have countless examples where I have been innovative and rendered initially expensive outlays unnecessary. This 'can do' attitude, honed from my experience, has helped me fashion a strong sense of self-belief. The reference points come from my own experience. For many, being made redundant would have been a significant blow. For me it provided the momentum to create my own business - a venture in which I have never been happier.

Future skills

Technological awareness

I have been involved in IT for more than two decades now. The changes I have seen in that period have been nothing short of incredible. If anything, advances in the next ten years will come at a greater rate. For any career, therefore, I would argue that technical awareness will be crucial to success. This will be true primarily in two areas: employing technology to streamline your existing processes; and, identifying emerging markets to break into.

E-commerce is a great example of where technology used correctly can speed up a process. It gives your business a competitive advantage and your customers better service. Think of a website selling shoes. Five years ago the owner would have been responsible for managing demand against his or her inventory, taking payments and ordering new stock. The growth of supply chain applications can now directly link customer demand to your inventory. Put simply, the website application knows when to request more stock by the number of customer orders placed. You may think this is small point, but in a business that processes five hundred orders per day this level of automation can reduce costs and free up time significantly.

The challenge of new technology also forces your business to evolve. When I first broke into the IT sector, DVD was the next big thing. It is more than likely that DVD will be phased out in the next ten years, as movies and programmes are streamed straight from the internet to Smart TVs. This change will revolutionise how consumers use and pay for their media. Already we are seeing growth in mobile payments and near-field technology. This will most likely render the use of cheques and credit cards defunct, raising in turn the challenges of secure payments, greater access to the market place and higher expectations of customer services. To remain viable and competitive, those operating in this marketplace will have to provide solutions to these challenges. The ability to see beyond the curve will be key.

Managing risk
Related to the technological advancements is the concept of change. Being an entrepreneur it is your responsibility to manage risk effectively. But how can you do this? First, it is not that complicated and boils down to financial common sense. When I first became self-employed in the media production business I started by buying a camera that allowed me to do the job but, more importantly, was also one I could afford. As my business developed and I acquired more capital, instead of buying fancy cars or clothes I put the lion's share of this money back into my business, bought better equipment and marketed myself more effectively.

Being an entrepreneur is not about taking wild risks. If you continue to play a high stakes game by either concentrating your capital in one area or leveraging your debts heavily against your assets, you will eventually lose. As the 2008 financial crisis showed, no individual or organisation can accurately predict the future. Spend only what you can afford. If you do need to borrow money, make sure the debt is serviced in a structured way in that you have predicted with some certainty that the business it will bring in further down the line will cover all related costs *and* provide some profit. Again, your expertise and experience in your business area will help you anticipate these areas.

One final word on managing risk. If you have never came across the terms 'leveraging debts', 'capital' and 'assets', do not worry. Financial literacy – simply understanding the basic concepts of money, business, and investment – is something that is poorly taught in schools. The good news is that these cornerstones of business are not hard to learn. There are many books, websites and short videos on YouTube to help you understand these core concepts. I will stress, however, that if you are to be a success in business you must not only understand these concepts but master them. This will come from both knowledge and experience. Fortunately some schools offer an experience of this through Young Enterprise programmes. This is a great way to get hands on experience of business and mastering some of the skills I have mentioned including managing risk and using technology in business.

Conclusion

Do not be afraid to be different. I enjoy the success I have today precisely because I chose to follow my *own* path. It is so easy to become caught up in the group mentality that you run the risk of losing the idea of self: understanding who you really are and what makes you happy. I was fortunate that I had the courage to follow my instincts from an early age. I would encourage any school leaver or career changer to do the same. You are far more likely to be a success by being true to your own interests and beliefs, because it is from here that your passion to persist and commitment to excellence will be drawn.

Do not be afraid to venture out of your comfort zone. Some people take a straight path in their careers and work through the formal route of higher education and employment. For me my education has been slightly more curved. You may not appreciate it at the time, but every job or task you do will provide you with a learning point that you can draw upon later in your career. The range of duties I fulfilled in the supermarket gave me the self-belief that I could successfully negotiate any challenges that came my way. When an opportunity to move into another career arose I was therefore confident that I could make it work. Similarly, when I was made redundant I knew I could be a success being the owner of my own business.

Above all, make sure that in whatever task you undertake your attitude is correct. People and situations tend to reflect back what you give out, so make sure you are positive and true!

Chapter 8
The Care Sector Executive

Ruth Smyth works in the care sector and is director of a well-respected nursing agency. She has won Fife Women in Business (FWB) awards for Most Enterprising Business and Outstanding Contribution to Business; became the Association of Scottish Businesses' (ASB) finalist for Outstanding Contribution to Business; and, was the Institute of Directors' (IoD) regional finalist for Director of the Year.

Ruth is also a keen Rotarian and was the president of a local Rotary branch. Rotary International is an organisation that attempts to bring together business leaders to provide humanitarian services, encourage high ethical standards and help build goodwill and peace in the world. Rotary's primary motto is "Service above Self." Ruth's own story shows how business can provide essential services for others.

When I was a young girl, probably around nine or ten years, I was given a book one Christmas entitled "Born to Nurse". The story about a young student nurse in Victorian England inspired me and from then on I always wanted to be a nurse. I began my nursing training at the old Royal Infirmary of Edinburgh and finished it in West Lothian at Bangour General Hospital. After I moved to Fife in 1982, I undertook my midwifery training, then left that particular avenue of nursing to have my two children. Returning to work, practice nursing led me down the road of academia as I was encouraged to undertake a BSc (Honours) in advanced nursing practice. I was proud to be one of the first nurse practitioners in Scotland working in general practice.

In 2000 I took up the position of manager of a fifty-four bed residential and nursing home. One early problem we encountered is a challenge that many businesses face - that of recruiting staff. In our case, our difficulty lay in recruiting agency nursing staff. Our second problem was attracting staff who were skilled enough to be able to do the job effectively. I wanted agency staff who were as committed to delivering an excellent standard of care as I was.

In December 2000 I incorporated Paramount Care Nursing Agency and for thirteen years I have been a director of this award winning nursing agency. Our aim is to provide an excellent standard of care at an affordable cost. Our main clients are local authorities who have to care for people in their own homes, privately funded home care and specially established care homes.

The provision of healthcare in Scotland is on the increase because people are living longer and wish to spend their later years in their home environment. The challenge that care agencies face is recruiting sufficiently large numbers of care staff who are either suitably trained or able to be trained in the necessary core values and skills needed to meet all clients' needs. We need more care workers to come forward and be trained in readiness for the expected rise in numbers of people aged sixty-five years and over.

There are lots of opportunities in the care sector, but to be successful you need to have the right skills. It is my belief that *commitment*, the *ability to plan*, priding yourself on *perfection* and having *a business mind* are all vital to being successful in this sector. I also believe that having integrity, building and maintaining a strong network, and always learning are vital skills for the future in this and any other sector.

Skills for success

Commitment

Working for a nursing agency is not a nine-to-five job. It takes a committed and caring workforce to ensure that all our clients receive the care they deserve and expect so that they are empowered to live as full a life as possible in whatever setting they find themselves, be that a care home or their own home. It is important that clients are properly assessed so that appropriate care can be planned and nurses or carers whose skills and knowledge match the client's needs can be assigned. Care is not just sitting down with someone, stroking their hand and wishing them well; it is carrying out intimate personal care, listening to harrowing stories of illness, family and life, and still being able to go in with a smiling face to the next client. Care is not just a job but is a commitment to making a positive difference to the lives of our clients.

Gaining and retaining knowledge about the person, his or her different ailments and possible treatments forms a fundamental part of the job. It is this information that helps care workers to plan and deliver simple or complex care measures for each client. Making sure that the information is accurate and reliable is therefore vital, and for this to happen there needs to be trust between the care worker and the client. Trust is often built when people show commitment to one another. That is why commitment is so important in building strong client relationships. The principles underpinning the National Care Standards in Scotland are dignity, privacy, choice, safety, realising potential, and equality and diversity and these are the principles that underpin all care provided by Paramount Care.

We all develop commitment in different ways. Often, following your passion is the best way for this to happen. Many people will do great things because they are committed to a cause, a job or a person. When I tried to get into a nursing school, I was met with several obstacles: I did not have the 'A' levels that had became necessary following changes to entry standards; I could not go to Northern Ireland because I had an English accent (those were the days of 'the Troubles'); and while Scotland seemed to be the only place that would take me, it would mean leaving home.

I only applied to one school of nursing in Scotland, and that was the Royal Infirmary of Edinburgh. I was committed to gaining a qualification and a job. Moving home and living somewhere else to achieve that was therefore not only something I was also committed to doing, but in itself served me well in the long run. Not only did it strengthen my commitment but it also tested me in many of ways and helped me to develop several other new skills. I have no doubt that moving away from home also helped me as a person.

Planning ahead

I have often looked back and wondered how I ever managed to get the agency off the ground. At the end of December 2000, my marriage failed and I was made homeless. I worked part-time in a GP's surgery, inputting medical records to a computerised system, and had only clothes and a car (still being paid up) to my name. I managed to get a flat to rent after a few days, thanks to a landlord who trusted me after only one meeting and allowed me to pay my rent monthly in arrears with no deposit. I never defaulted on a payment and was so grateful to this man for giving me a chance.

At the beginning of December, together with a friend I had started putting together a plan for the nursing agency. A range of skills came to the fore at this time: risk-taking, initiative and sheer determination. We had incorporated the company and had equal shares. We had gone to my bank manager to ask for a loan to set up the business. He had listened carefully to what we said, and told us that he would do some research into nursing agencies and give us a decision at the beginning of 2001. We also went to the Small Business Gateway offices in Glenrothes and spoke to an advisor there. Finding and taking advice are essential for anyone if they are to do well in the modern workplace. There is a lot of help out there for starting up in business and you should seek it out. Programmes like Young Enterprise are great for developing your skills in school. After school you can find support through organisations such as the business gateway or local business associations. Books like this are also great for sharing ideas and advice on how to achieve and be successful in your field.

Starting up, for the first time I found myself encountering terms such as business plans and financial projections. We had to learn fast. We sat and listened to our advisor before hurrying home to work out on paper what type of customers we were aiming for. There was a lot more to consider. What prices did we need to charge in order to pay staff? How could we make sure the prices were right while leaving a bit over for ourselves? Where would we work from? All these questions had to be answered in our own minds before we could formulate our business plan. Having ideas is great, but they need to be thought through and planned out.

Now it was January 2001 and I had to go back to my bank manager and explain that I was living in a small flat, with no money and a car on hire purchase. He said that he believed I knew my sector (nursing) and that his research had shown that money could be made from nursing agencies. He also appreciated my honesty in telling him what was going on in my personal life. He already knew my financial situation. He asked how much money I would need to set up and so I gave him our business plan and asked for £3,500. This would cover our office rental for three months, and other sundries such as stationery and advertising, phone and internet costs. He gave me a loan of £7,000 with no strings attached. I had no property or assets to use as collateral anyway. It was a personal risk but, in business, you need to take some calculated risks.

Then problems arose within the agency. My co-director and I had differences of opinion on many levels and went our separate ways. Working with only one administrative assistant resulted in me having to go into the office at 6am each day and leave well into the evening. It also meant that I had to find a great deal of money to give my co-director. I had no idea the legal wrangling it takes to buy someone out of a business. I would advise anyone who is going into business with someone else to ensure they have an exit strategy in place at the start. When starting a business no one wants to think about it ending. However, having this in place is a great safety net and can save a whole lot of pain in the long run.

I lived a life of panic, worry and desperation, but that only made me more determined to continue what I had started. I just had to grit my teeth and get on with it. As well as paying off my co-director I had legal expenses to pay, and some weeks I wondered where the money would come from. Businesses took around six weeks to pay our invoices. One week I needed just over £2,000 to pay the staff, but there was no money. The situation brought me to my knees and I prayed for some to come through. My administrative assistant and I were amazed when a cheque came in for the amount we needed plus a few pence extra, allowing me to pay my staff on time.

Planning equals perfection
Getting it right when caring for others, or in business, is no accident. Success and achievement come about when plans come together. Planning is needed to achieve perfection.

I have been a perfectionist ever since one particular episode in my early working life. When I first left school I worked in a lawyers' office and was secretary to one of the partners - not bad for a first job! In my keenness to please, I typed up letters so quickly that I was often pulled up by my boss for returning her letters with mistakes in them. At seventeen years old that was a hard lesson for me: I had to stop doing things so quickly, and check my work at each stage to ensure that it was legally correct and accurate. The fact that there were no computers added to my frustration, because if I made a mistake typing legal documents on parchment I had to start again. I soon was able to produce work that was perfect, and when I was asked to look after the petty cash and keep a simple spreadsheet of expenditure, I was thrilled.

These days it is not a legal partner who scrutinises my work, but the Care Inspectorate for Scotland. This body was formed under the Public Services Reform (Scotland) Act 2010 and is the independent regulator of approximately 15,000 services. The Care Inspectorate comes to our offices at least once a year to audit our care provision and staff recruitment, and to ensure that I have the necessary legal framework and insurance for my care business.

Prior to the inspectors' visit I am required to complete separate questionnaires for the nursing agency side of the business and for the care at home side. I must also complete a self-assessment online again for both sides of the business. Much of January and February each year has to be set aside to complete these mandatory tasks if we are to be allowed to continue providing care. Whilst they are onerous and very repetitive tasks, it does give me confidence knowing that the care sector in Scotland is being carefully vetted to ensure that vulnerable and needy people are receiving the best care. Each agency is scored and their results posted on the Care Inspectorate website so that potential and current clients can view them.

At any time the Care Inspectorate can carry out unannounced inspections, and I continually advise my staff that the company – both office and care parts – could be scrutinised at any time of the day or night. The Care Inspectorate also sends out questionnaires to my care staff and clients asking for feedback about the company, its management, the training and the care provided. The people being questioned are picked randomly, so we really have nowhere to hide, and both good and bad practice can be picked up. I am proud of the fact that our scores have increased year on year. I believe that this is due to carefully recruited care and administrative staff who have bought into our strapline, 'Paramount Care – where CARING comes first'.

The financial side of a business is often something you either embrace or hate. Either way, you cannot get away from it and it is important that you know what your financial situation is at any time. As my business grew, I went from working with spreadsheets on which I itemised all my incomings and outgoings, to using more sophisticated accounting and payroll packages. HM Revenue and Customs (HMRC) is unforgiving if you make mistakes. I found the local HMRC office's training programmes interesting and enlightening when I started out. It made me think about things I had never considered, such as statutory sick pay and maternity pay. None of my staff had been sick or pregnant up to that point, but I was at least ready for the first employee who was. All the training was free, which is a huge bonus especially when you are just starting up.

I now am in a position to employ someone to carry out the financial transactions of the company, but because I have done this myself I still have a good understanding of what is going on and can have intelligent conversations with my accountant. Instead of being directed by someone outside the business, e.g. the accountant, I can have an informed and fruitful discussion so that my goals and expectations are met legally and financially.

My nursing agency has grown over the years, from being managed in a one-room office to now being run from a large office in Fife and a smaller one in Edinburgh. All this has been achieved by very hard work on everyone's part. By constantly reviewing where we are, where we want to be in the next three or five years and what our charges and pay rates are, and by asking everyone to buy into our strapline, 'Paramount Care – where CARING comes first', we are all striving to make the agency the best in the UK. Office staff meet at least weekly, and during this time they review clients, staff, training and any challenges brought to their attention that can be dealt with immediately. This provides a safe environment in which confidential items can be put on the agenda, for where there is honesty and transparency there is less likelihood of tensions arising in the workplace. Care home managers also gather together at regular intervals and discuss the quality of care agency staff and make recommendations.

As a result of all this, the business has an excellent reputation. Nor do we need to advertise for clients because as satisfied people talk to their relatives and neighbours, word soon spreads.

Business acumen

My father was a manager in a small, gents' outfitters shop in Fife before becoming an evangelist travelling all over England and Scotland. I was only six years old when he made that major lifestyle change. Nevertheless, I can remember the passion he had for the small shop, his pride in the way the clothes were hung on rails or laid out in drawers and most of all, his pride in his customers. They were all given special treatment by him and the shop flourished under his management. There was only one other person in the shop to help him. On his half-day off each week, I used to go with him to 'help' tidy the drawers and learn how to wrap the same pair of socks or a tie over and over again until my packages were considered good enough for customers. My mother did not work once they were married, but she had been a bookkeeper and secretary for a linen factory for many years.

During my break from nursing to have my children and before I took up my position as practice nurse, I worked in my husband's picture framing shop. For a while the shop was not making money. There I learned about everything needed to run a successful business. I learned that knowledge of the products and our competitors was crucial: it was not about simply undercutting everyone else's prices. I also realised the importance of keeping up with current legislation on payroll, VAT and accounting practices: with budgeting virtually non-existent we were continually taking out more money than we took in, never taking into account overheads and what money we needed simply to feed and heat our family. I was able to draw on all these experiences of bad practice to make sure that the nursing agency was run ethically, morally and efficiently, with customer needs and preferences taking priority. Money drives business, but so does truth and honesty as I have found out over the years.

As you can see, I had no formal business training before I started my own business. However, probably because of my strict moral upbringing I wanted to make sure that everything I did was legal and within the restraints and constraints of the regulatory bodies, e.g. the Nursing and Midwifery Council and the Care Inspectorate for Scotland. I attended training sessions on so many topics, including VAT (value-added tax), PAYE (pay-as-you-earn tax), NI (national insurance) and Intellectual Property, and kept my continuing professional development up to date so that I could continue to practice as a nurse. When I started out, I attended everything that was free because money was tight. These days I can afford to be choosier and handpick the courses that will be advantageous to me personally and to the business. I do, however, direct my management team and administrative staff to courses that I think would be suitable to their line of work.

To be the 'registered person' for a nursing agency in Scotland, that person must be a registered nurse. As I stepped back from the business, it was crucial that my manager was also a registered nurse. This has made a vast difference, in that I can trust her to carry on the day-to-day running of the agency along the same lines as I did. I know that she will look at care from a nursing perspective, and that she will give staff clear instruction on what care each client requires and how that care should be delivered in accordance with national care standards.

Skills for now and in the future

Integrity
Having previously worked in a care home and used agency nurses when short-staffed, I knew the other nursing agencies and their managers. I knew the prices they charged and, by speaking with the nurses and carers they sent into the homes, I knew what they paid. I knew how they recruited their staff and what training, if any, they delivered. This gave me a good starting point for setting up my own nursing agency because I could make sure that my staff were better trained and paid a tiny bit more, and I could charge below the going rate for trained nurses and carers.

I also decided that the business would be based on truth and honesty in all that we did. Should someone phone for staff, we would be honest and tell them whether we had someone available or not. Too often I had waited for an agency nurse to appear at the start of a shift, only to be informed subsequently that the agency did not have anyone available. We also asked for honesty from clients: if they were contacting other agencies too, they were to let us know as soon as someone was provided so that we could stop searching for someone.

Agency staff are employed by us on a permanent, zero-hours contract. This is because many have other jobs and because the varying nature of the care required at any one time by our clients means that we cannot guarantee always to give them work. When we first started out, it took us three months to get enough staff together so that when care homes started contacting us we could supply staff to them. I was honest with all applicants and told them the situation: we needed them to sign up with the agency but we did not yet have the clients who would generate the work they were signing up to do. These same carers and nurses stayed with us until the care homes to which we had sent out advertisements came to us looking for staff. We still have those care homes and some of those carers and nurses on our books.

Truth and honesty are important in today's job market and are key to being successful and achieving. I have no doubt that this will still be the case going forward into the future. They are fundamental values that all people need to be successful in themselves and with others, as it is after all others with whom we work, whom we serve and whom we benefit from being with. If there is a breakdown in these values the consequences often result in bad publicity, which leads in turn to loss of business.

Networking

I have a great circle of friends, many of whom I gained through networking. Networking is an excellent way of meeting like-minded entrepreneurs when you start out in business. At networking events you can share stories of good days and bad days, and talk about what worked for you and what did not. Some also have speakers to give guidance and insight into how to 'do' business.

Fife Women in Business (FWB) is a group of women who come from all areas of business. Initially I was in awe of many of them because they seemed so professional and successful. Yet I went on to become president of FWB and treasurer of the Association of Scottish Businesses (ASB), which launched me further into different networks where I met people who have motivated, congratulated, advised and stood by me. I would like to think that I have done the same for others.

Networking has mushroomed over the time I have had my business, in particular through social media sites where most businesses now have a presence. Instead of going out to breakfast, lunch or evening networking events, I can use sites like Facebook, Twitter and LinkedIn to share what I am doing and what the business is achieving, in real time. However, there is nothing like talking to someone face-to-face, where tone of voice and facial expressions can help to enhance the communication. I came to realise that walking into a networking event where I do not know anyone can be less daunting if I remember that everyone else is there for the same reason as I am - to promote themselves and their business. I found that a smile helped to break the ice and that talking over a drink or some food often relaxes everyone.

Dena Kouremetis, an American freelance copywriter and author, is of the opinion that attending meetings is better than social media networking for business. To some extent I do agree, although you have to be willing to dedicate time and money to join and attend meetings, and then be committed to making the meetings work for you. It can take several months of attending networking groups before people begin to remember you and you start to build up trust, especially with larger groups.

According to an article in the Daily Mail on 13th June 2013, fifty-seven per cent of UK residents use social media. It therefore made sense for me to set up social media pages for Paramount Care, with links to and from our website. A very high percentage of my staff use Facebook and Twitter, so I also regularly use them to inform staff about what is going on in the company and point them towards training and other organisations that may be useful to them in their personal or professional lives. I am also able to 'follow' people and companies that are in the same professional field or whom I think it may be advantageous to connect with. Social media is a great way of sharing information quickly. Nevertheless, in many cases once it is out there it cannot be taken back, so you must be more careful about what you are saying on these sites. Unlike with face-to-face conversations, you cannot easily correct or clarify what you have said.

Lifelong learning

Lifelong learning is a vital skill to take with you wherever you go. In order to meet the requirements of my nurse registration with the Nursing and Midwifery Council, which allows me to practice as a nurse, I have always had to prove that I have undertaken continuing professional development (CPD) by attending courses or reading journals, etc. Now that I am director of Paramount Care, I do not carry out practical nursing but teach and direct my staff in order to enhance their skills and knowledge. I must therefore still keep myself updated on business and financial legal frameworks, and ensure that my management team knows about current care practices, medical treatments for clients and employment law.

All registered nurses must undertake CPD in order to remain on the register of nursing, and I expect all Paramount Care nurses to make sure that their CPD portfolio is up to date. We are able to view a nurse's registration online in order to check that it has not lapsed. When carers working in Scottish nursing agencies have to be registered with the Scottish Social Services Council (SSSC), as will be the case in the next few years, they will have to complete a nationally recognised qualification to allow them to work as a carer. I have always believed in training my staff, and in 2012 Paramount Care was accredited by the Scottish Qualifications Authority to deliver SVQs in Health and Social Care. This means that staff can not only take pride in working for an award-winning agency, but can gain a recognised qualification that proves they have the knowledge to underpin the practice.

Conclusion

Last year I was asked by an ex-neighbour to be her business mentor. I feel very privileged to be able to guide someone else through the legalities and responsibilities of being a chief executive officer in business. We are learning together and so it is mutually beneficial.

I have also opened a second office in Edinburgh. It is bringing back all my memories of when I started up in business back in 2000-2001, although this time I hope to do it without all the mistakes I made along the way. Learning from mistakes has been a large part of my success. However, I am blessed to have an excellent management team who think like me, have great business acumen and integrity and who, most importantly, are determined to make a difference to people's lives. Together we all seek to provide care for those who so often are lonely, sick and needy. Achieving that goal is a great motivator and requires great skill.

Chapter 9
The Third Sector
Recruitment Executive

Alan Surgeon is an Edinburgh-based entrepreneur with over ten years' experience of working in the voluntary sector. He is the owner of AWS Charity Recruitment, a specialist recruitment agency that focuses on fundraising jobs and executive searches for registered charities throughout the UK.

His agency, which supports the Institute of Fundraising, has won several awards for outstanding customer service.

I have always wanted to be my own boss. From an early age I always felt I was a leader and not a follower.

Despite this, at school I never really knew what I wanted to do with my life. I would have meeting with teachers and careers guidance advisors who would simply add up how many 'A', 'B' and 'C' passes I achieved in my exams and then map out the rest of my life for me according to what they thought was best. It was also common to hear comments from teachers like, 'Your older sister is good at this, so why don't you try it?' Who were they to know who I was and what I wanted to do? The art of listening seemed to be absent, something I have noticed from high school to this very day. You gain a huge amount from people just by asking simple questions and listening. It seems very simple but the two lessons I drew from those school experiences were these: careers education is not straightforward; and, listening is just as important as talking.

This early uncertainty about my career was, however, a blessing in disguise. Not knowing what I wanted to do, I threw myself into various part-time jobs whilst studying at school and later, university. It was a great way to learn a lot about various different jobs and gain the experience that would help me to choose a longer term career path. My first part-time job was in retail, and it proved to be probably the most beneficial learning experience I had. It was here that I learned how to work as part of a team and how to be disciplined in observing working hours and rotas. Most importantly, it was in retail that I learned the importance of good customer service and good communication - two skills school does not necessarily equip us with. Work experience also boosts your confidence. For example, if you are not that great at public speaking, being confronted with the public every day is a great way to develop that skill and boost your confidence. Working in retail I was engaging with the general public, dealing with lots of questions and sometimes having to go away to find the answer for them. It was a steep and beneficial learning curve.

One thing that was not so great, however, was witnessing the lack of work-life balance amongst my colleagues. I noticed very early on that a number of people seemed to be off work for long periods of time with stress, depression, anxiety, and other physical or mental health conditions. I remember thinking, 'Why is this?', and vowing never to fall into the same trap myself.

These and other key behaviours were to become vital parts of my own eventual working life: ensuring that I balanced work with social life; continuing to learn; learning from others and networking; developing business acumen; a willingness to diversify; and, building a well-respected reputation. Each would prove just as important to my career as would having appropriate subject knowledge and experience.

My skills for success

Achieving a work-life balance

The answer to why my colleagues were suffering long-term illnesses was simple: the vast majority had no work-life balance. I will give you an example. My first experience of retail was with a well-known, high street store. Here I experienced a wide variety of different management styles, which is a fantastic learning experience for anyone. We would work long hours in the store – 9.00pm starts and 6.30am or later finishes. We were also expected to work an extra twenty minutes on either side of the shift (unpaid) to help 'replenish stock'. Including travel time that could mean a thirteen-hour plus working day, and as a result people were basically burning out.

Working on and off in that store while I was studying, I was able to observe at first-hand how a lack of work-life balance can wear people out and affect their physical and mental health. The key question it raised for me was, was is it worth it? In my opinion, without family, friends and a social life we do not work at our best. Life outside of work brings a host of experiences and skills which can help us in our work and vice versa, and friends and family have a crucial role to play. Maintaining a work-life balance is a great achievement in itself and should not be overlooked or undervalued.

Volunteering and lifelong learning

Although it may seem counter-intuitive, it is often not until after our formal school education that we begin truly to value learning and education. Whilst still at school but working part-time I decided that I wanted to go on to study at university. Unlike most people, or so it seemed to me, I opted to study something I enjoyed. If we find things we enjoy then we often enjoy learning about them. I chose the subject I did because it was a hobby of mine, even though it was unlikely to lead me to becoming the next Lord Sugar! I always knew that I wanted to help people and this, combined with a desire to understand how the human body works and how to look after it, led me to read alternative medicine.

It was during this time that I first decided to do some volunteering with a project in Edinburgh. I cannot recommend volunteering highly enough. It is a brilliant way to enhance your skill set and ideal if you have a specific area you want to improve on, such as administration, working with the public, events, fundraising or public speaking. The equivalent of taking on lots of different part-time jobs, it broadened my horizons, allowed me to meet lots of people and helped me to develop lots of new skills.

While volunteering I found out about a new health project that was looking to recruit new staff to start a few months from then. I had more or less finished studying by this point and had decided, as a result of my positive experience of volunteering, that I wanted to work with charities. The project also appeared to promote alternative medicine, which was of course the subject I had studied. I looked up the job description for administrator and was disappointed to discover that I did not meet all the role requirements. Fortunately for me, though, the organisation was more concerned with finding someone with the 'right personality' as opposed to a broad range of experience and knowledge. I therefore set about trying to make my CV look more attractive than those of candidates applying with a business administration degree or extensive experience in the area. I did so by drawing on the breadth of experiences and skills I had already gained up to this point.

I learned so much from this process. I cannot emphasise enough how important it is to tailor your CV to the job you are applying for. In my current role I know that only too well, but this was a great first lesson in how to make my unique experiences fit and sound attractive to a prospective employer. Job descriptions are useful for identifying potential candidates, but making sure that someone is the right fit for an organisation is vital. Often qualifications are not proof that someone can do the job. Always remember that skills and evidence of lifelong learning, coupled with drive, determination and a keenness to achieve, go a long way. In my case, taking a range of voluntary and part-time jobs developed and honed the range of skills I could bring to a job.

The upshot was that within a few months I was employed in my first 'grown-up', 'proper' job and on a career path in the voluntary sector. Since then I have worked in a range of jobs in the charity sector, from administration to finance to running my own business, all of which have further boosted my experience and skills base. The "Shift Happens" videos on YouTube are so true - the future workforce will have up to fifteen or more jobs in their lifetime and so will continually need to keep learning and relearning!

Communication skills

During my time working on the health project I developed a passion for organising events and marketing. Marketing is basically communication skills for a company. It is about getting others to see, hear and understand the value of your product or service. It was a lot more difficult when I first started: without Twitter, Facebook or LinkedIn I actually had to speak to people! Through time I have learned about using social media in marketing, but even this is changing and I find myself constantly having to relearn how to communicate effectively in the modern world.

Another vital communication skill I developed was empathy. I was working with a variety of vulnerable people, some of whom were very unwell and in some cases dying. I was still continuing with the alternative medicine side of things. Indeed there ended up being quite a few crossovers between this and my other roles, as I helped to co-ordinate both a successful complementary therapy programme and a launch event to promote its programme of activities. I was also heavily involved with events and fundraising. I really did enjoy this part of my job and began to think seriously about pursuing a fundraising/events position or something to do with communication and marketing in the charities sector.

Always remember: any job you have is experience, whether it is packing boxes or working in a legal firm. Thinking to the future, take what you can from it. As you will see from my career history, each experience I had opened my eyes to new things and took me in a different direction. What becomes clear to me throughout, though, was that no matter what job I worked in it was important to have good communication skills.

A willingness to diversify

At this point in my career I continued to want a bit of everything: business development, fundraising, events, communication and marketing, complementary therapies, and, working with charities. So I got the best of all worlds by taking a job with another charity and setting myself up in business! The charity sector job came with slightly more responsibility and a national remit. It also used more of my skills. At the same time I began working as a self-employed events professional, promoting alternative health through events and roadshows throughout Scotland.

Although I was doing two jobs at the same time, this was no bad thing. Having the breadth and volume of experiences I had gained from all my part-time work, volunteering and job placements helped me to diversify. Looking back there is so much I would have done differently, because not everything went to plan. In all the excitement of setting up on my own while working for someone else, I forgot a few crucial details. Lots of mistakes were made, but more importantly I learned from them. What I learned, can best be summarised as the need to have business acumen and budgeting skills - in essence, business skills (see below).

My charity work had by now turned me into an accomplished events/fundraising professional. I was therefore on the lookout for anything that matched my skill set. As a consequence, I went on to work as a fundraiser with two charities, one local and one national, giving me a useful dual perspective on the industry. All my previous experiences now came together nicely. For example, I was able to use my knowledge of alternative health when organising a fundraising event on the subject. Both organisations actively promoted alternative medicine and had a variety of programmes/treatment centres, so there had been an obvious link when I applied for the posts. During this time I also learned a great deal about working to targets with minimal supervision, and about motivating and inspiring supporters for the causes for which I worked.

I really enjoyed fundraising and events (and working with charities generally to help others), but a huge number of positions, especially in Scotland, tend to be on a contract basis. I had now reached a crossroads and was pondering my next move. I decided to register with a recruitment agency that dealt specifically with jobs in the charity sector throughout Scotland and Northern Ireland. By chance it was the agency director I spoke to because the consultant managing the 'Charity Desk' was on maternity leave. After my registration process I had what I thought was an informal chat about my experience. Following our conversation, however, the director called me back in and asked me if I would like to work with the company on the Charity Desk.

I had not expected this, nor did I know if I could 'do' recruitment. I knew the charity sector in Scotland and had worked for a number of different causes. I knew about organisational structures and I knew about administration, fundraising, events and human resources from my previous jobs, so I had a good understanding of the key roles and what they involved. The only actual thing I had not done before was recruitment. Nevertheless, I thought about the skills I did have - networking, working with others, a willingness to diversify, business awareness and acumen - and on that basis I took the plunge!

You are probably noticing that I seemed to end up in jobs that, on paper, I was not initially qualified to do. Nonetheless, for the first time in years I was now well paid (very well paid) because we worked on commission and received a bonus as well as our basic salary. Basically I managed the Desk as well as staff for the charity sector in Scotland and Northern Ireland. Yet again I had found myself a position that brought together my skill set nicely: my knowledge of the charity sector; the customer service skills I had used in retail; the business development experience I had gained from being self-employed; and, the all-important patience I had developed from the management skills I picked up along the way. Although the firm had a policy of rewarding talent, we had to work hard. Maintaining a healthy work-life balance was encouraged, though, and the culture of the organisation was very me. I can honestly say that if it was operating today I would probably still be there now, but sadly after just over a year of my working there it closed.

It is amazing how your career journey takes on a life of its own. You can only control the controllable, and ultimately you must be able to bounce back from setbacks you cannot control. After the setback of the company closing I decided I wanted to be my own boss again; I wanted to be in control of my own destiny. So that is what I did!

Business skills

Even in the charity sector you need to be business savvy. The following guidance did not come out of a rule book but is a list of advice I wish I have been given earlier in my life. It would have made my work life so much easier and enhanced my business in the early days.

- Have some cash behind you. Save up. Or, if you are luckily enough to be under thirty years of age you can get advice from the Prince's Trust, which also offers small start-up loans. In the current climate banks are reluctant to lend money to start-ups unless you have assets (once you start making money, though, they will be your best friend). Having a savings cushion is vital in case you hit a dry spell, are forced to work fewer hours or worse still, are off sick. It is also crucial not to have too much, if any, outstanding debt when you start out. Be very careful with credit too - it can get you into a lot of difficulties later on.

- Have a business plan that clearly sets out what you want to achieve in three, six, nine and twelve months. Setting goals and reviewing them is very important.

- Check out what legal guidelines might apply to your business. Is there a governing body whose codes of practice you must adhere to? Fees for legal advice can be expensive but they could save you a lot of money and trouble in the long run.

- Hire a decent accountant and be sure you register with HMRC (Her Majesty's Revenue and Customs) for tax and national insurance purposes. Everyone has to pay tax. As a business you need to know how it applies to you, so the sooner you find out the better. There are lots of places to find information – from websites to the great advice given by business gateway advisors.

- Keep things simple: do as much as you can to save money, but be realistic. For example, do you really need office space? Remember that you can work from home using a virtual office address to establish your presence until you have sufficient capital to rent office space.

- Put in the ground work yourself first, and do not take on staff unless you really need to and money allows.

- Stay disciplined and develop a routine for your working day even if you only work part time. It can be easy to do too much (remember what I said about work-life balance) or to find yourself busy doing lots of things that are not making you money (the so-called 'busy fool').

- Trust your instincts when it comes to outsourcing and be prepared to move if you are not happy with the products or services you are buying. I failed to take this advice myself at first, but I am now on my fourth accountant and have stopped wasting money on human resource specialists by using an employment lawyer.

Managing your reputation

Having had the opportunity to make mistakes and learn from them before starting my own business, I was in a better place to go it alone. There are always difficulties in getting a new business off the ground so it is essential that you establish a good reputation. Fortunately, through the relationships I had built up over the years I had a good name in the charity sector so work came my way quickly. Reputation-building is so important in any place of work. It can be developed alongside other skills, such as networking. Indeed you should take every opportunity you can to network, especially in person, because it is a great way to get business referrals. Even so, while networking is important, doing the actual job and doing it well is the best way to gain and maintain a great reputation.

Building good relationships with your external suppliers and finding ones you can trust is vital. Once you start asking, you will be amazed at the number of people you already know working in your area. With clients, always be patient no matter how hard this can be. Some people will take a long time before deciding to enter into business with you - something to remember when it comes to budgeting ahead - but good ground work and patience will pay off in the end. Most importantly, always treat others as you would have them treat you, be confident in your abilities and surround yourself with as many positive people as possible. There is a lot of negativity out there and it does no good to become immersed in it. Always be positive and look to the future.

Skills for the future

Networking

I have mentioned networking when discussing current skills, but I really think it is important to raise it here under skills for the future. Networking can not only be great fun, but it is also vital for personal development and the growth of any business. Cultivating business contacts and a client base will also be key should you wish at some point in the future to diversify into other areas.

Attending networking events is great for generating ideas, sharing your knowledge with like-minded individuals and seeing things from another person's perspective. You may also find someone who has been in the same situation as you at some point, so you can avoid future pitfalls by learning from other people's mistakes! I personally use these occasions to meet potential clients and candidates because they allow me to get to know people by speaking with them directly, in person. I am a true believer of the adage that people buy into people. For me nothing is more important than meeting clients face-to-face, because that way you really get to know each other and it makes doing business together easier in the long run. Even if you do not walk away from these events with business there and then, speak to as many individuals as you can, build a name for yourself and get your company brand known because referrals through word of mouth are often the best kind. With so many social media platforms available, people can stay in touch with you in a variety of different ways. The first step though should always be the initial face-to-face interaction. It is in this way that trust is born and connections made.

Networking cannot be overlooked as a key skill for the future. For that reason, if you are nervous about meeting and speaking to other people I would strongly recommend joining local clubs, groups or getting into volunteering to build up your confidence. If after that you are still daunted, the next stop would be to seek professional help. Schools, colleges and other groups all offer this kind of support.

Creativity and change
Creativity is not just about having artistic ability. Think about it: if you are thinking about starting up your own business or have done so already, then that involves being creative! Many of us have come up with really innovative and smart solutions to problems in our lives. As humans we are naturally creative, but we need to learn to harness our creative skills particularly if we are to thrive in the future workplace. The world has many problems but finite resources to deal with them, and so the employment market increasingly needs people who are able to generate creative solutions.

Developing your business over time also requires creativity, in order to be able to look at opportunities and problems in a new way and from different angles. Having good ideas and running with them is great. Some will work and others will not, but it is always good to get the creative juices flowing and it will do wonders for enhancing your entrepreneurial abilities in the long term. Having an idea is one thing but being able to implement it is another altogether, so do not be disheartened if an original idea does not work out as planned: it is all part of learning, and creativity is often a continual process.

It is also important to remember that being creative frequently necessitates change - a concept that many of us struggle to cope with. In the future workplace it will be vitally important to remember that while consistency is often regarded as a strength, change can also be good. Indeed change already seems to happen more often and more quickly in the fast-paced, modern workplace of today. My ideas, outlook and business plan have changed so many times over the years, but always for the better and invariably generating more activity and success. Thus, coping with change and harnessing creative juices to help make change for the better are, in my view, both vital skills for the future.

Building a strong team

Change cannot happen on its own. Creative ideas need to be shared with others if they are to work. I have said before, that my advice would be not to take on staff unless you have to. Nevertheless, in life your 'team' is always much bigger than simply those you employ. For me it also includes business contacts, charity links, friends and family. Building a strong team is key for any business to succeed and for any employee to achieve. Remember that your team, whether big or small, represents your company brand and supports you as an individual. If you have the luxury of being involved in recruiting members to your team, be picky and take your time when appointing staff. It is one of the most important decisions you will make. Yes, you will make the odd mistake along the way – who does not? - But recruiting the right staff is vital. So too, is training and motivating staff. It helps to retain the good ones and can be one of the most rewarding parts of your work. Being able to include team members and encouraging them to share ideas is a fantastic way of developing your business, especially as your staff are often the ones closest to your clients and therefore more in touch with their needs and views.

Depending on the size of your business, it can also be a good idea to build good relationships with professional advisors in the following areas:

- Accounting and finance: it is more than likely that you will need some kind of book-keeping support. A good accountant will keep you informed about your financial situation and advise you on relevant matters of tax and finance legislation.

- HR/employment law; if you are at the stage of hiring staff you will need to draw up employment contracts. My advice would always be to consult an employment lawyer for this and for keeping up-to-date on employment law.

Conclusion

There are so many things to take account of when starting out. Many of my fellow contributors to this book seemed to have a clear plan in place when they left formal education, but do not be too concerned if you do not. A good way to find out what you might like to do and enhance your skill set at the same time is by volunteering and engaging in third sector work. Try to do things you enjoy, but cultivate the ambition to grow into different positions too. Remember that it is okay for an idea not to work; just stay focused and try again. Your path may change but remember that skills are transferable so have confidence in that.

I have always worked in the charity sector in some capacity. Even now I am still fundraising. The main difference is that now I am advising on job descriptions and how to pick the ideal candidate rather than applying for jobs myself - but having the knowledge that comes from being on the other side of the fence has been invaluable. I have always stayed focused and determined, and I have welcomed any opportunity to learn and taken advantage of any training that came my way.

Being your own boss is fun, but I would advise anyone, self-employed or not, to do the following: keep learning; do some charity work; build a good reputation and respect all with whom you come into contact; build good teams; and, most importantly, keep a good work-life balance. That is my key to achievement. If you are able to take on board just a little bit of each contribution to this book then the rest will come naturally.

Chapter 10

The Military Officer

Paul Wilson is a former major in the British Army. Prior to that he was a commissioned officer in the Royal Navy. For a period he was the youngest lieutenant in the fleet and won awards for Best Academic Performance and Best Officer Under Training. Specialising in intelligence, Paul has served in conflict zones around the world such as Afghanistan and Iraq. He has briefed military and civilian leaders at the highest levels of government, including U.S. General David Petraeus and the British ambassador to Afghanistan.

Drawing on his diverse intelligence background, Paul now works as a security consultant for the largest professional services firm in the world.

Success has always been difficult for me to define, but I surmise a true reading to be when all seems to be 'going well'. For me that is certainly true as I write this. I have had a successful twelve-year career as a commissioned officer in the British military: eight years in the Royal Navy and four years in the British Army Intelligence Corps. After myriad interesting roles I am now a security consultant for a large professional services company. I will not be writing this article with misty-eyed yearning for the romance of the often interesting work I undertook during my time in the military. Nor will it be a guide on how to be successful. Instead I hope it will prove an interesting vignette of my experiences and what success means to me.

I joined the Royal Navy as a lieutenant three days after leaving university, some four years ahead of my peers. As a twenty-one-year-old, who looked slightly more bedraggled than the average, I was put in charge of large teams. The challenges were numerous but I took more positives from the opportunity and developed as a person. After eight very quick and enjoyable years, during which I undertook a number of intelligence roles, I was recruited into the British Army Intelligence Corps where a successful career in British intelligence resulted in me leaving as a major only four years later.

In this article I will try to convey three key tenets that led me to a sense of doing 'well' and hence to my own brand of success. I will also describe the characteristics that I myself try to embody, and share what I have learned from strong, fair and universally accepted 'successful' leaders in the military, central government and, most recently, the private sector.

First, though, I want to give you some background on why I joined the military. Was it because of family ties? A sentimental sense of duty to Queen and country? No – it was purely down to the experiences and opportunities afforded me whilst in the Sea Cadets. I joined the Sea Cadets aged eleven, as a slightly awkward, gangly 6'5" beanpole who stooped and had little confidence. I was bullied at school – little wonder given that I was taller than most fully grown men. Thankfully it did not take the form of systematic, physical bullying by those bigger than me (as no-one really was). Instead I was subjected to subtle, emotional abuse, which left a lasting impression on me. When I joined the Sea Cadets I was wet shaving, my side burns belying my tender and impressionable age. I left, a 6'7", confident, adventurous and personable man, forever thankful for the military bearing, leadership and team skills I was taught.

My exposure to the regular forces throughout that time allowed me to realise opportunities to work as a team in very interesting and varied places with like-minded people. The Royal Navy was always the right fit for me, and romantic notions around the fictional James Bond as a Royal Navy commander only pushed my eleven-year-old ambitions further in that direction. So it was that aged twenty-one, having successfully studied and socialised my way through university, this lad from a state school in the Midlands - incidentally not far from the most inland point in the UK - joined officer training at Britannia Royal Navy College as the youngest lieutenant in the fleet.

During my career I received awards for Best Officer Cadet and Best Academic Performance, going on to hold senior positions of authority and responsibility at a much earlier age than that of my peers, without doubt because of my Sea Cadet training. I have not looked back since.

Three key skills to my success

When it came to writing this chapter I canvassed peers, friends and colleagues about the three key things they thought were the drivers of my success. Despite some initial banter involving more comic characteristics, their answers thankfully (and weirdly) aligned with my own.

Likeability

The first skill or characteristic is likeability. I have worked with some prickly, socially awkward, even demonic people, and I have worked with some exceedingly sociable, relaxed and gregarious people. With whom did I prefer working? - the latter, for sure. Would you not? Being a junior officer charged with managing a team of thirty-two sailors (most of whom had been in the Royal Navy longer than I had been alive) meant that I had to be flexible, understanding and knowledgeable, all of which are part of being likeable. I have led numerous teams throughout my career, and feedback from those involved suggests that likeability was at the forefront of my success. Indeed formal feedback revealed that for many I was the best manager with whom they had worked.

Praise indeed or just a splattering of misplaced sycophancy to me? Knowing the people giving the feedback it would not be the latter. Military people generally are not deft at passing subtle criticism or praise. There simply is not the time to pussy-foot around because ultimately people's lives are on the line. This realisation, the continual positive feedback I received plus the existence evidence of a team I took pride in nurturing and leading, drove home the importance of being a personable and likeable individual.

During my latter assignments in military intelligence, I had to rebuild or sometimes even establish relationships with counterparts in the other countries' intelligence organisations. Given the nature of their role, intelligencers (intelligence officers) are generally quite closed, calculating and suspicious of everyone. Being approachable, open, honest and sociable helped me to break through those barriers and reshape obstacles into opportunities. For example, during my time in Kabul, Afghanistan delivering strategic intelligence to senior civilian decision-makers in the UK and USA, the flow of intelligence was improved because of my personal relationships with key interlocutors across different intelligence agencies. Five years on these relationships are still going strong despite my no longer being in the intelligence game. This may be why a large number of my roles have involved establishing processes, doctrine and hard-wired relationships as a liaison officer to numerous organisations.

Equally though, a point of warning: likeability is a double-edged sword. From experience I have learned that some people may try to exploit you. Being open to people in order to try and get the best from them also opens you up to people who may get close to you and try to mislead you. As a manager, being consistent in all that I do means people know that if they cross a certain point there will be ramifications. Being likeable should never be mistaken for weakness or a sign that someone can be taken advantage of, and it is important to establish boundaries early on. A further note of warning: being over-the-top and too much of a 'joker' will detract from your professionalism. There is, as ever, a balance to be struck which will come through experience. Remember that what you should be striving for is 'leadership' not 'likemanship'.

Vibrancy
My second skill is vibrancy. One of my senior managers in the military (who is now one of my closest friends) once wrote an annual report about me with the line, 'Paul is a radiator and not a drain'. When I first read this I was perplexed, but then I understood. I have always thought vibrancy to be one of my key traits. Positivity exudes confidence and a warm personality. Even in times of adversity and high-pressure environments I have always tried to exude an air of vibrancy. Sometimes this has belied my true feelings, but in order to lead

teams through tough situations without wavering and maintaining positivity even when things really are difficult, inspires people to follow you.

During my time in Afghanistan I led a team with forever changing priorities, all of which were critical. We were under-staffed and operating on minimal sleep - and when I say minimal I mean two or three hours a day. Something had to give. Tensions were high and tempers fraying. Misjudged vibrancy would have done little other than annoy the team. I therefore had to tailor it to a more appropriate level. I always communicated with my team, making sure that they were aware of the reasons behind changes, giving them the opportunity to ask questions and providing support where necessary. Doing so enabled us to function as a cohesive and reliable unit: we were all in it together. I managed to maintain their waning morale by funding an endless supply of sweets and pizza. When the madness around us subsided to a more manageable level, I made sure that we all got together for a period of relaxation (this was war, so it meant one night watching a film together with non-alcoholic beer and a late start the following morning). I personally debriefed everyone on a one-to-one basis and expressed my gratitude to them. This transparency, positivity and honesty, got us through some increasingly difficult times together as a team.

Vibrancy to me means that you can operate on different levels. Being a source of positive energy means that you will attract like-minded people and even more energy. Ultimately ask yourself who would you rather follow: a dour, miserable person or someone who radiates vibrancy and is good fun?

Commitment

My third attribute is commitment. I think in all honesty that this comes from my upbringing, but commitment is the thread that also runs through my previous two points. Whether it is to friends, doing a job well, your school, your course or company, commitment is paramount. It goes hand in hand with consistency. People will know what you want and what they can expect from you if you show commitment to getting the job done and are consistent, while as per my previous point, being transparent allows people to know why, what, where, when. Commitment gives people the confidence to rely upon you on a consistent basis. In the military, such individuals were described as being 'fire and forget' people. This complimentary term refers to a weapons system, and means that the individual can be given a task and then relied upon to complete it to the highest standard.

Importantly, a key to my success has been my commitment to the teams that I have not only led but been part of too. I have always maintained that I am only as successful as my team is. Building rapport and team spirit is fundamental. Do it early and do it well. It is often too late to forge lasting relationships when the heat is really on and you are unsure of people's capabilities and how they will react to different stresses. A prime example of this was when I was leading a small, disparate team of specialist counter-intelligence professionals. We were all on different tasks across the world. On the rare occasions when we were all in the office I made a point of getting us all out for a 'phys session' (a very military thing to do – usually a run or hill-walking laden with weights). More often than not we would go for a bike ride, our plan being to travel forty or so miles in one day. In reality, we would hit the nearest pub for a 'toilet stop' where we would remain for the entire afternoon. The unifying camaraderie of the exercise resulted in me taking a fundamentally broken team and making it one of the best, to the point where others became keen to join.

Success in the future marketplace.

The working environment I have known since my weekend job at sixteen, being in the military to now working in the private sector, has changed enormously. The fundamentals are the same, in that professional and positive people invariably do well. Nevertheless there are three elements that I think are crucial to ensuring that you continue to be at the leading edge of success, whatever the marketplace.

Soft skills

As a trained interrogator it is my opinion that soft skills and human intelligence (HUMINT) remain fundamentally important despite having become less prominent in recent times. This is because in spite of the continual erosion of traditional working routines and office-based work, human interaction remains crucial even if it does have to take place remotely.

The correct use of the English language through spelling, grammar and syntax was hammered into me by the military. Its importance is even more apparent in the private sector. Writing is the most common way of communicating a request or providing the information necessary for someone to do their job successfully. Writing using the ABC approach has worked well for me: A – Accuracy; B – Brevity; C – Clarity. Taking time to reduce complex language, using the minimum number of words needed to get your message across without detracting from it and being consistent in your use of language will give you credibility and make you an effective writer. Senior officers in the military do not have time to read pages of a report. They need the 'bottom line up front' (known as the BLUF), which means concisely summarising the most important points and putting them at the very top of the report so that they can be absorbed quickly and easily. Always write succinctly, breaking up your text into easily readable sections, avoiding unnecessarily long words and using headings and subheadings to guide your readers to the information they are looking for.

Another soft skill that I believe will contribute to success in the future is that of neuro-linguistic programming (NLP) - the clever and subtle use of words, syntax and mirroring body posture to get people to change their behaviours. NLP is not black art, but is a skill set that can help you to achieve what you want and be alert to others who may try to exploit you. It can also help guard you against bias, and thus can be a crucial skill for anyone who is part of or leading a team.

Agility

Remote working sounds great to most people: the ability to tailor your own schedule, working in your own comfort zone whilst hammering out emails and nipping downstairs for proper coffee that does not cost the earth. To me, although working from home is a good thing it is peppered with difficulties that stem primarily from the fact of managing a team you cannot see. In the military, this difficulty was further compounded by having to send people to areas of the globe with limited means of communication. In such instances, the personal agility and preparation of each team member for every possible hurdle enabled them to deploy with both ease and the confidence of knowing that they were fully armed with all the facts and tools they needed to do the job successfully. The same kind of preparation and support can be seen in the training, guidance, support, and access to information that is readily available in the private sector.

I currently work in the technology realm. Change here happens rapidly to say the very least. Keeping abreast of developments will make it easier for you to seize any opportunities that arise. Being adept at changing direction and keeping on top of changing contexts and requirements means that you can get through more work, thus adding even more value in your workplace. Practise this by taking on more extra-curricular events and saying 'yes' to more opportunities than you do currently. I once spent a whole month saying 'yes' to everything. It made for a very expensive and tiring month, but is an experience I have been feeding off ever since. Be warned: it is equally important to know when to say 'no'. No matter how agile and able you are, there may be times when your workload is such that something has to give. Just make sure that it is not your health! It is important to identify and realise your priorities. Managing your own time is the first step to becoming a successful manager of large and disparate teams.

The University of Life and the World around us

Being interested in the world around you shows that you are neither single-minded nor a one-trick pony. Immersing yourself in it will help you to stand you out from the crowd and give you the confidence and experience that can only be garnered by getting out there and doing it – whatever 'it' may be. The world is converging, and being more aware of different cultures, approaches, company development and politics will give you better insight into why things are the way they are. Demand for diversity in the workplace will only increase with time. Having a girth rather than a dearth of experience makes you a more rounded person and will further help you to be a part of and lead large teams.

My motto has always been, 'we're here for a fun time, not a long time'. Get out there and have as many positive experiences as possible. Be in control and shape difficulties into opportunities. Join a sports team, whether it is a running club, squash league or five-a-side football team. Join a pub quiz team. Broaden your social group and keep those who really resonate with you, close. Always be intrigued by the world around you, be open to new things and say yes to new things that will give you a wealth of experiences.

Conclusion

I hope you see my chapter not as the ramblings of a mad man but as a frank article about where I think I have fared well and why. Although the narrative of what 'success' looks like is a little muddied, I do believe that my three separate, but interlinked, tenets have stood me in good stead.

To some it may seem that I took the easy option, joining something I knew a lot about, but being away from friends and family for months on end was in my view the harder decision to take. Luckily I found different friends and a new (military) family. I would sincerely recommend the military to anyone. Yes, it has occasional frustrations, but so does every walk of life and I believe that the opportunities for growth and development it offers are second to none. When I left it was because the timing was right for me to do so. I had experienced all I had set out to and believed that there was nothing more that it could offer me. My new company has continued to give me the adventure, intrigue, responsibility and support I enjoyed in the military, in a seamless transition.

Never give up on your own dreams. Sometimes they may seem impossible and unrealistic, and sometimes the timings might not fit, but keep hold of them until that one day when everything comes together. Remember - the only measurement of success you need to gauge your achievements against is your own.

Paul Wilson is a pseudonym so as to protect the real identity of the subject of this case study.

Chapter 11

The Painter and Decorator

Barbara Hastie started work as a painter and decorator at the age of seventeen. Since then she has worked in both small and large companies as well as on her own. She has taken part in many national competitions, including Dulux Apprentice of the Year and SkillBuild regional and national finals, and is well-respected for her work on a national level.

She has owned her own company and now teaches the next generation of painters and decorators through her role as a college lecturer.

I have always been a great believer in 'what is for you will not go past you'. On the other hand I also believe in 'what we do determines our own fate' and 'you only get back what you've put in.' I truly believe that you can have faith in all these statements. Some things in life you cannot control but other things you can. Life is very much like a bank. The best thing you can invest in in the bank of life is the development of your own skills. The more skills you can develop and enhance, the better your skills will be in learning, life and work.

It is quite daunting to be in my thirties, looking back at what I have achieved and how I got to where I am today. Through reflection I would put it down to a passion for my work and love of being creative. It is also the result of determination and taking on lots of lifelong learning. Without a doubt, finding something you enjoy and being able to keep refining your skills are key colours in the art of achievement.

Finding my passion and igniting my creative skills

I left school at sixteen because I could see no further progression for me there. I enrolled in a business course at my local college, not because I really wanted to but because there was no other option at the time. All my friends seemed to be more 'intelligent' than me and stayed on to do their exams. On my college course I took away one lesson: I did not want a career in office administrative work. I had a placement doing that one day a week and hated every minute of it. I needed to do something different.

Before I got the chance to do something different, life's events took over. As the youngest in my family I was utterly devastated when my mother passed away from a terminal illness. She was my best friend, and I was now the only female in a male-dominated household. It was hard at first, but it gave me a good grounding in working in male-dominated environments which would serve me well in the future.

My father was a self-employed heating engineer, and had always been self-employed from the day he could work. His father was a plumber to trade and ran a successful local plumbing company till the day he retired. My second oldest brother worked as a joiner, again self-employed as soon as he could be. My oldest brother worked in the local builders' merchant serving the trades. Family connections and experiences have a massive influence on career choices. Sometimes this is a good thing and at other times it is good to look beyond what has always been. The possibilities of my career being in trades seemed sealed in many ways even though I was a girl.

In the weeks that followed my mother's death, my Dad took me working with him so that he could keep an eye on me. My father, my brother and I spent that summer renovating a property they had bought. Putting a full dormer conversion on top of a second story flat became my major task. I quickly came to enjoy the work. I loved getting my hands dirty, stripping off the old slates and clearing and carrying timber, and just to witness the whole transformation of the building had me hooked. I could use my creativity and loved seeing the whole project come together stage by stage. I went home with a sense of achievement; I had created something everyone could see. It was a real buzz.

Until that point no-one had ever mentioned that I could work in the trades – it was just not an avenue girls went down. I thought about being a joiner but disliked the splinters I frequently got from the wood. Plumbers were always getting wet, as were plasterers, and 'brickys' worked outside a lot and because I hated the cold that was a no-no too. I chose painting and decorating because I enjoyed art at school. I now saw houses and rooms as a larger canvas - it was just that the brushes were bigger. So with a renewed purpose in life I trotted back to the same college and enrolled in the full-time painting and decorating course.

From the moment I put on the overalls I felt I had found my 'something'. Painting and decorating is a very visual trade. We are the last to leave any job and our work is the first visual thing clients see when they walk in. We are the ones that make all the other trades look good. As someone once told me, 'You can only tell a good joiner by the good painter that followed them.' This is very true. We are the ones covering up the mistakes and making them look good at the end.

I was the only female on the course but it did not deter me one bit. My tutors treated all students the same. I did everything the others did, and probably tried to be even better at the outset just to prove that I was there for the long haul and could do just as good a job as the guys, if not better.

Determination

To continue in the industry you need to be employed by a local company under an apprentice scheme. In a small local area, finding a job in a very male-dominated industry was no mean feat. I knocked on many a door with no success, but through the help of my lecturer I found a local company with eighteen employees (a large company for the area) that was willing to give me a trial period and work on a placement basis.

It was hard at first. I can still remember my first day standing out in the cold at the front of the workshop at 7.45, waiting for everyone else to turn up. Out of the eighteen men only two spoke to me that morning. I had many a second thought as the week went on but I was determined to stick it out and not let any of them put me off. Yes there were snide comments, but from my upbringing I knew how to give as good as I got. More importantly, I wanted to prove to them that I could do the job just as well as them if not better. My hard work and determination paid off and I was signed up to the CITB (Construction Industry Training Board) apprenticeship scheme. I still remember the day I had to sit the entrance test and walk into a class full of men (potential joiners, brickys and painters) – it was a show-stopper but I carried on regardless and passed the test.

My apprentice years were spent mostly on new build works, with a few private jobs thrown in. I worked on cold building sites for months with over eighty men and as the only girl on site. There was no running water and only two portaloos - nor were they male and female! Thankfully sites have changed a lot over the years. My fellow tradesmen and I became good friends. I loved the camaraderie of working with the different building trades. We did a lot of work for a large local circuit manufacturer. It involved twelve-hour shifts day and night to complete the work on time. I was working ten metres above chemical corrosive baths, washing acid off beams before re-coating them. It was not very nice work but I still enjoyed the sense of achievement I got when the work came to an end and I could see the finished effect I had created. This was what kept me coming back for more and sticking at a job I had come to love.

Over the course of my apprentice years and through my time spent at college I was given the opportunity to compete in local and national painting and decorating competitions. In these environments I would work alone within a set time to produce a test piece of work incorporating the skills I had learned both at college and 'on the tools'. The majority of these competitions were single entrant where I competed against other apprentices from across the country. I was quite successful at them and found that I worked well under pressure. It was a great experience to travel the country, to see the other colleges and know that the finish I was creating was good enough to win at national level. I received the 'Best Painting & Decorating

Apprentice of the Year' award in 1995 from my college and won a holiday voucher. I took my then boyfriend, an electrician, on that holiday. Years later he became my husband. We both look back upon that holiday and remember well the delight I had in winning.

At the end of my four-year apprenticeship and after gaining my SVQ and Advanced Craft City & Guild award with Distinction, I was starting to look for more specialised roles in my profession. I was determined to unleash my creativity and looked for wallpapering jobs, domestic painting and private work. I bumped into a boss of another local company and he offered me a job. I jumped at the chance because I knew that this company specialised in the kind of work I wanted to do.

Since then I have travelled in the back of cold vans for hours to get to jobs, worked in large hotels and beautiful private historic houses, hung very expensive wallpapers and worked closely with interior designers. People thought that was it was strange that as a female I wanted to be the one applying the paint rather than giving the advice on interior design. This spurred me on and made me more determined to prove them wrong and do an even better job.

Doing it by myself - self-determination
Two years had passed working in my specialist role and my feet were getting itchy again. I was seeking my holy grail of being a respected, self-employed tradeswoman and proving that I could work and run a business on my own. So in the summer of 1997 I bought a little van and set up my own painting and decorating company – Barbara J. Davidson - Painter & Decorator. Many people were dubious but I was well used to negative criticism by now and was determined to prove them all wrong.

I successfully ran my own company for five years. Specialising in private work, with my main clientele being women, I received great feedback on my neatness, finishing and polite manner. I also gave helpful advice about the best wallpapers and colours to choose. I did all my own bookwork, budgets and accounts, pricing jobs and settling bills. I did my own tax returns and got to grips with areas of business that I would never have excelled in at school. Doing it on the job and with the purpose of doing it for myself made me even more determined. I worked on interior and exterior work and was driven my love of the trade and a determination to succeed.

Lifelong learning

During my self-employed days an advertisement appeared in the local press for a part-time lecturer in painting and decorating at the college where I first gained my qualifications. I instantly recalled my college days and how much I had respected my lecturers. I thought that if I could pass on my enthusiasm, skills and knowledge to future generations and encourage more females into the industry by my mere presence in the trade I would feel more fulfilled in life. Learning had been so important to me, and I was guided and encouraged by so many people in the college I hoped I could do the same for others. I felt I would be giving something back to a trade that I loved. I went through the interview process and got the job.

The times that followed were some of the toughest times I had career-wise, as I was still working at my own business as well as trying to learn teaching skills. It is only once you have to explain something to someone else that you realise how important it is to educate others. I ended up working 'on the tools' all weekend to compensate for my time spent preparing lessons at the college, and spent my nights either studying myself or looking again through teaching material for my classes. My first days of teaching were a little bit surreal. I remember having the same feeling I had when I put my overalls on for the first time: I felt I had found my new 'something'. To be able to teach a skill to individuals and to see them get the same gratification from it that I did, and to encourage and support them along the way by drawing on my own experience, was deeply rewarding.

I taught part-time for nearly two years. When a full-time position came up I applied for it successfully, wrapped up my business and concentrated on teaching. I decided not only to teach but to get the proper qualifications and learning I needed to be the very best at teaching others. I worked towards a professional development course in teaching and then a teaching qualification in further education through Open University courses. When teaching you are constantly striving to raise your skills and knowledge through certification. For me that door is never closed, and I still find myself working towards different awards to enhance my teaching. I can highly recommend gaining additional qualifications to anyone who needs to improve their skills and qualifications in any area.

Getting my various teaching qualifications was not bad for a girl who had left school at 16 because she felt she was not clever enough - determination and lifelong learning rolled into one. This is what I try to pass onto my students. You can always go back and do whatever you want. You may have left school with no purpose or focus, but the door is always open and it is what you choose to do with opportunity that counts. My dad never at any point said to me, 'You can't do that', but always said, 'You can be whatever you want to be so long as you are happy in your choice.' As I found through the years, his advice was good. I also learned that you get back what you put in.

I try, whenever possible, to take students through to national competitions. I find that competition has the same effect on them as it did on me, in that it breeds enthusiasm and confidence in their abilities, both in their trade and as individuals. I have had a few success stories as well over the years, with some students even competing at international level.

Where I am now
I have now been teaching for thirteen years. I married the boyfriend whom I took on my prize-winning holiday and helped him become self-employed. We now have two children and I am still teaching. Most recently, I have been appointed external verifier for painting and decorating with the Scottish Qualifications Authority (SQA). The work involves visiting other centres that are delivering SVQ awards in painting and decorating and checking they are meeting SQA requirements and that standards are maintained. I enjoy this work very much because it allows me to meet fellow lecturers from different centres and see how they deliver their awards. I still get a few raised eyebrows when they see that I am a woman, as the area is still quite male-dominated, but I can definitely see a change from when I first began teaching.

Future skills

There are lots of skills that are important in our trade, and as I said above I really think that determination and lifelong learning are crucial. If I was to think about skills for the future I would say that there is one factor to consider above all others, and that is personal fulfilment. Working in trades is a people job, and being able to make people happy is vitally important. Along the way you need to make yourself happy too. I have found that I am happiest when others are happy. Giving something back is therefore the one thing I would encourage others to do in the future, no matter in what career they find themselves.

Giving something back – returning your investment
I still love my trade. I love to be 'hands on' when I get the opportunity (which is rare with two small children). I love being on site and the camaraderie that exists with other trades people.

Every new student who comes through the workshop brings with them their individuality. I still thrive on seeing them develop their skills, supporting and helping them to win that elusive apprenticeship which will see them develop in time into well-rounded individuals. I occasionally meet some of my former students and I enjoy nothing more than hearing how their careers have developed. Several have taken their skills abroad, having emigrated to places such as Australia, New Zealand, Canada and Scandinavia. To know that I have had a hand in their success spurs me on to help future generations, including my own children, on their career paths. If they too can give something back, then the art of achievement will continue.

Looking ahead I can see that the future workforce will need certain key skills. Some that I have found to be crucial for success in the trade are *good communication, planning* and *time-keeping,* all of which are underpinned by teamwork.

Communication
Communication with customers, fellow tradesmen and women, and suppliers is generally achieved via telephone or face-to-face contact. Getting it right in the first contact you make is paramount. If you cannot get the basics right you will not be able to grasp fully what it is clients are looking for. It is also vital to maintain contact, so phoning back people immediately and keeping them informed of progress against deadlines are also important habits to adopt.

Planning
Being able to record information accurately and plan work effectively is something that is essential when work gets busy. I have found through my teaching career that some of these skills are being lost because of more and more reliance on multimedia and text messaging. Some students coming to college find recording and planning skills hard to maintain and build upon. Nevertheless I persist in pursuing them because they provide valuable grounding for work in the real world. There is no cutting corners when it comes to good planning. Plans need to be accurate and sufficiently detailed so that from the start everyone - you, those working alongside you and the client - is clear on exactly what is required to complete the job. The level of detail this requires cannot be conveyed by texts.

Time-keeping

The final skill that I touched upon above is time-keeping. In my teaching job I am never late for a meeting - I'll be the one sitting outside well before starting time. It was working in my trade that honed my attitude to time-keeping. Holding up a job means lost earnings, so you must be on time. This is all the more important for big jobs when teams are working together. Here if you are running late it is not just yourself you are holding up but the other six men as well. This costs money and is a sure-fire way to frustrate your boss and, quite possibly, your chances of continued employment! Good time-keeping is something that can be built on from school. In fact timekeeping, along with communication and planning, are attributes that follow you throughout life and can have a very big impact on success on your chosen path.

Conclusion

Achievement truly is an art. Just like painting and decorating, it involves brining lots of different paints together and ensuring they creatively hang to get the final picture or design you wish for. Lots of things will influence that achievement. Some of them can be life changing negative events. For some this will be the end of their journey and their goals will seem unachievable. For others this will be the catalyst to even greater success and achievements. Amongst it all determination is vital. However you need to know what really motivates you and what your passion is before you use your energy. Be clear on what you want to achieve and ensure that you learn along the way. By mixing all of this experience together you will be one step closer to making your life a masterpiece!

The End of the Beginning

'We shall not cease from our exploration, and the end of all our exploring will be to arrive where we started and know the place for the first time.'

(T. S. Eliot)

Your career is an exploration of yourself. The success you enjoy in your career is a reflection of your thoughts and actions. How badly do you want to achieve? How much time and effort are you willing to commit to your endeavours? Do you really believe you can be a success? These are questions that will shape your career and can only be answered by you.

The remarkable finding from reading every chapter in this book is how the career journeys of such a diverse a group of people can have so much in common. What we see first is the identification of an area of excellence - for Barbara Hastie, for example, this was decorating. We then see a significant setback countered by the determination to carry on - for international athlete Jayne Nisbet this was her eating disorders and her triumph at overcoming them. Finally, we see a self-acceptance and recognition by these individuals that through their hard work they do deserve to be at the pinnacle of their profession - for Blair Nimmo this was becoming one of the youngest partners in the history of KPMG.

In terms of our own learning, therefore, what can we take from the career stories of our contributors? Clearly, success is rarely a straight line but rather a curved path with more than a few bumps in the road! The parents of Keith Girdwood did not send him to a private school so that he could stack shelves in a supermarket. Nevertheless, through this experience he found the best 'education' for him, and set himself on a course that would lead him eventually to found his own successful media company.

It is also clear that our contributors would not change their path. Angela Davidson talks of the importance of resilience in her role as a paediatrician. It is difficult to envisage how resilience can be built up without being brave and placing yourself in positions where you are testing skills for the first time, under great pressure and faced with the prospect of failure. Successful people, however, embrace this type of challenge because they know it is the most effective way to hone their craft.

The 'extra-curricular' path of our contributors is also a common theme. Leslie Vella talks of the importance of 'Saturday jobs' and also of developing his interpersonal skills of meeting and working with people whom he would not otherwise have come into contact with on his path to tourism. Similarly, Nicola Stanley-Wall in her journey to becoming a microbiologist speaks of her volunteering work as having been crucial to her ability to manage the move away from home at an early age. Again the key aspect here is confidence in being able to interact with others and make friends easily. Alan Surgeon also benefited from volunteering because it gave him great responsibility at a young age and provided valuable insight into what career path he should take.

Moving to the future, it is clear that for many of our contributors being able to get the most out of technology is becoming increasingly integral to their roles. In her position as a nursing agency director, Ruth Smyth emphasised the concept of 'lifelong learning' as being crucial to maintaining excellent levels of service. It is evident that the concept of technology as a tool of efficiency will be applicable to every human endeavour. Keith and Nicola both mention the importance of mastering this area in the modern workplace.

Interestingly, many of our contributors see a commitment to giving something back to their local community as a key theme of their future careers. For Blair Nimmo this has taken the form of KPMG's support for the homeless charity 'Shelter' and many other local projects. Similarly, the celebrated chef Craig Wilson has worked tirelessly for cancer charities. It is clear in most of our case studies of success, businesses of the future and successful people within them will only be truly successful where they have a mutually beneficial relationship with the community in which they are located.

To return to the quote of T S Eliot, you may ask how this applies to skill development? The business skills of Blair Nimmo, the craft of Barbara Hastie, and the expertise of Craig Wilson – these skills were already present in each individual from a very young age, even if they initially failed to recognise this themselves. The key to each of their journeys was to develop to a level of excellence through determination and commitment to their chosen field – and to continue to pursue their goals no matter what obstacles they faced. Thus your end too will be found in your beginning, so make sure your first step is a good one!

Neil McLennan & Kevin Murphy

Further reading:-

A blog has also been set up to share further learning about the skills for success. More information on the success stories of contributors can be found at this site, which also gives information on how to contact the authors of this book.

http://www.determinedtosucceed.edublogs.org   (Short link www.bit.ly/skills4success)

More details on KMPG can be found at:- www.kmpg.com

More details on the Scottish Training Federation can be found at:- www.stf.org.uk

More details on Jayne Nisbet Personal Training can be found at:- www.jnpt.co.uk

More details on Eat on the Green restaurant can be found at:- www.eatonthegreen.co.uk

More details on the University of Dundee can be found at:- www.dundee.ac.uk

More details on the Malta Tourism Authority can be found at:- www.visitmalta.com

More details on the NHS can be found at:- www.nhs.uk

More details on Media Voodoo can be found at:- http://mediavoodoo.co.uk/

More details on Paramount Care Nursing Agency can be found at:-
http://www.paramountcare.com/

More details on AWS Recruitment can be found at:- http://awsrecruitment.co.uk

More details on being an officer in the military can be found at:-
https://www.gov.uk/government/organisations/ministry-of-defence/about/recruitment

More details on Borders College can be found at:- www.borderscollege.ac.uk

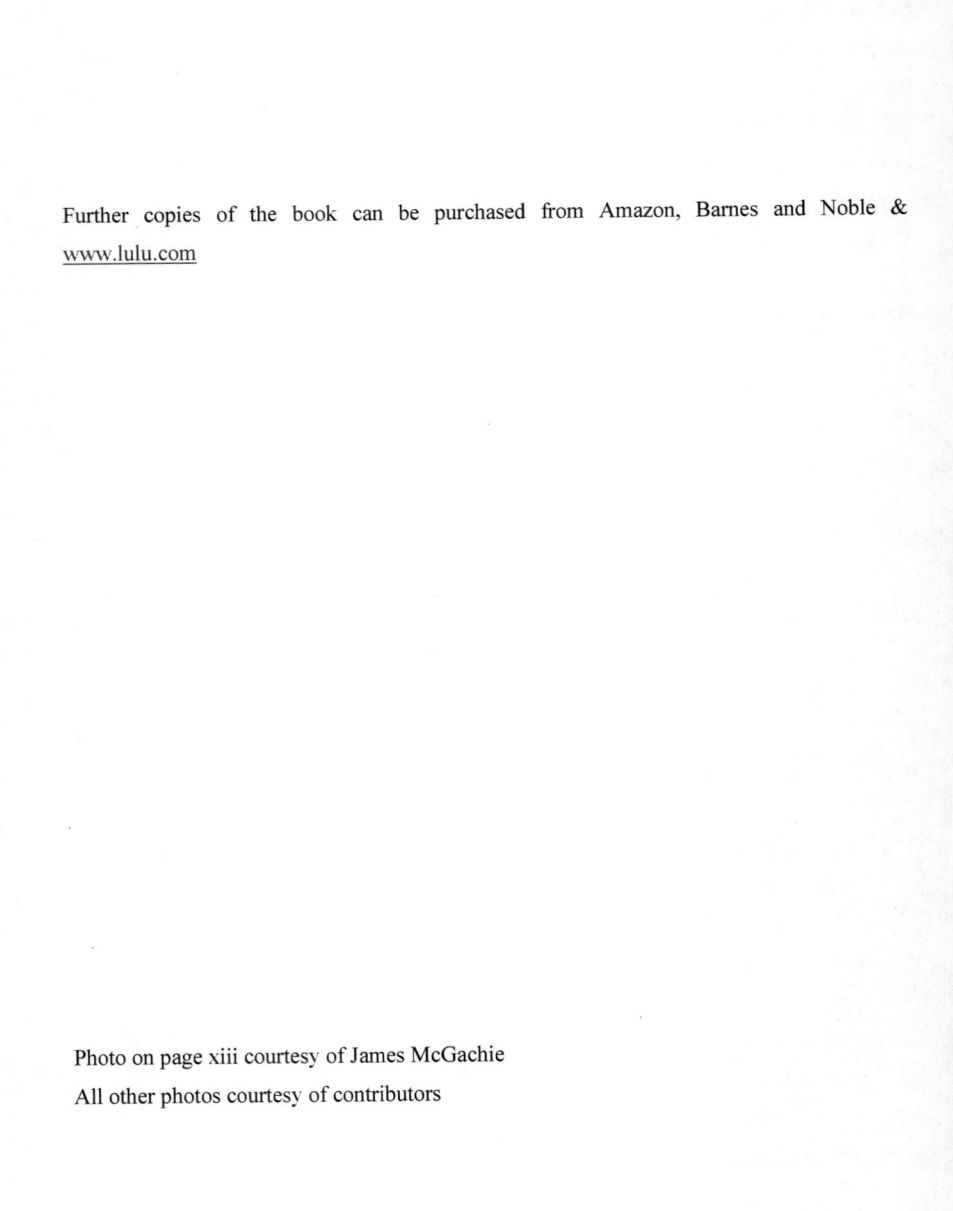

Further copies of the book can be purchased from Amazon, Barnes and Noble & www.lulu.com

Photo on page xiii courtesy of James McGachie
All other photos courtesy of contributors